THE CONSERVATIVE NANNY STATE

How the Wealthy Use the Government to Stay Rich and Get Richer

By Dean Baker

Published by the Center for Economic and Policy Research
Washington, DC

Published by the Center for Economic and Policy Research
1611 Connecticut Ave., NW, Suite 400
Washington, DC 20009
202.293.5380
www.cepr.net

Cover design by Paper Cut Design

ISBN: 978-1-4116-9395-1

CONTENTS

PREFACE _____ v

INTRODUCTION _____ 1

1   DOCTORS AND DISHWASHERS: How the Nanny State
    Creates Good Jobs for Those at the Top _____ 17

2   THE WORKERS ARE GETTING UPPITY: Call In the Fed! _ 29

3   THE SECRET OF HIGH CEO PAY AND OTHER
    MYSTERIES OF THE CORPORATION _____ 39

4   BILL GATES – WELFARE MOM: How Government
    Patent and Copyright Monopolies Enrich the Rich and
    Distort the Economy _____ 47

5   MOMMY, JOEY OWES ME MONEY: How Bankruptcy
    Laws Are Bailing Out the Rich _____ 59

6   THE RIGGED LEGAL DECK: Torts and Takings (The
    Nanny State Only Gives) _____ 67

7   SMALL BUSINESS BABIES _____ 77

8   TAXES: It's Not Your Money _____ 83

9   DON'T MAKE BIG BUSINESS COMPETE AGAINST
    GOVERNMENT BUREAUCRATS _____ 91

CONCLUSION _____ 103

REFERENCES _____ 109

ABOUT THE AUTHOR _____ 113

PREFACE

This book is written in frustration and hope. People in the United States who consider themselves progressive must be frustrated over the extent to which conservative political ideologies have managed to dominate public debate about economic policy in the last quarter century. Even when progressives have won important political battles, such as the defeat of efforts to privatize Social Security, they have done so largely without a coherent ideology; rather, this success rested on the public's recognition that it stood to lose its retirement security with this "reform." It also helped that the public was suspicious of the motives of the proponents of Social Security privatization. However, success in the goal-line defense of the country's most important social program is not the same thing as a forward looking agenda.

The key flaw in the stance that most progressives have taken on economic issues is that they have accepted a framing whereby conservatives are assumed to support market outcomes, while progressives want to rely on the government. This framing leads progressives to futilely lash out against markets, rather than examining the factors that lead to undesirable market outcomes. The market is just a tool, and in fact a very useful one. It makes no more sense to lash out against markets than to lash out against the wheel.

The reality is that conservatives have been quite actively using the power of the government to shape market outcomes in ways that redistribute income upward. However, conservatives have been clever enough to not own up to their role in this process, pretending all along that everything is just the natural working of the market. And, progressives have been foolish enough to go along with this view.

The frustration with this futile debate, where conservatives like markets and progressives like government, is the driving force behind this book, along with the hope that new thinking is possible. We shall see.

I appreciate the assistance of many in the writing of this book and the conversations that led up to it. The most important people in this group are my colleagues at the Center for Economic and Policy Research. Several people gave me helpful comments and feedback on earlier drafts. This list includes Michael Meeropol, Lynn Erskine, Marcellus Andrews, Mark Weisbrot, Heather Boushey, John Schmitt, Robert Johnson, Katherine McFate, and Helene Jorgensen. Since this book draws on many books and papers written over the years, the full list is much longer, but in the interest of brevity and the fear of excluding good friends, the others will remain un-named. I also thank Helene, Fulton, and Walnut for their immense patience.

The Government vs. the Market

A Useful Political Parable for Conservatives

Political debates in the United States are routinely framed as a battle between conservatives who favor market outcomes, whatever they may be, against liberals who prefer government intervention to ensure that families have decent standards-of-living. This description of the two poles is inaccurate; both conservatives and liberals want government intervention. The difference between them is the goal of government intervention, and the fact that conservatives are smart enough to conceal their dependence on the government.

Conservatives want to use the government to distribute income upward to higher paid workers, business owners, and investors. They support the establishment of rules and structures that have this effect. First and foremost, conservatives support nanny state policies that have the effect of increasing the supply of less-skilled workers (thereby lowering their wages), while at the same time restricting the supply of more highly educated professional employees (thereby raising their wages).

This issue is very much at the center of determining who wins and who loses in the modern economy. If government policies ensure that specific types of workers (e.g. doctors, lawyers, economists) are in relatively short supply, then they ensure that these workers will do better than the types of workers who are plentiful. It is also essential to understand that there is direct redistribution involved in this story. If restricting the supply of doctors raises the wages of doctors, then all the non doctors in the country are worse off, just as if the government taxed all non-doctors in order to pay a tax credit to doctors. Higher wages for doctors mean that everyone in the country will be forced to pay more for health care. As conservatives fully understand when they promote policies that push down wages for large segments of the country's work force, lower wages for others means higher living standards for those who have their wages or other income protected.

Conservatives don't only rely on the nanny state to keep the wages of professionals high, they want the nanny state to intervene through many different channels to make sure that income is distributed upward. For example, conservatives want the government to outlaw some types of contracts, such as restricting the sort of contingency-fee arrangements that lawyers make with clients when suing major corporations (conservatives call this "tort reform"). This nanny state restriction would make it more difficult for people to get legal compensation from corporations that have damaged their health or property.

Conservatives also think that a wide variety of businesses, from makers of vaccines to operators of nuclear power plants, can't afford the insurance they

1

would have to buy in the private market to cover the damage they may cause to life and property. Instead, they want the nanny state to protect them from lawsuits resulting from this damage. Conservatives even think that the government should work as a bill collector for creditors who lack good judgment and make loans to people who are bad credit risks (conservatives call this "bankruptcy reform").

In these areas of public policy, and other areas discussed in this book, conservatives are enthusiastic promoters of big government. They are happy to have the government intervene into the inner workings of the economy to make sure that money flows in the direction they like – upward. It is accurate to say that conservatives don't like big government social programs, but not because they don't like big government. The problem with big government social programs is that they tend to distribute money downward, or provide benefits to large numbers of people. That is not the conservative agenda - the agenda is getting the money flowing upward, and for this, big government is just fine.

Of course, conservatives don't own up to the fact that the policies they favor are forms of government intervention. Conservatives do their best to portray the forms of government intervention that they favor, for example, patent and copyright protection, as simply part of the natural order of things.[1] This makes these policies much harder to challenge politically. The public rightfully fears replacing the natural workings of the market with the intervention of government bureaucrats. This stems in part from a predisposition not to have the government meddle in their lives. In addition, the public recognizes that in many cases the market will be more efficient than the government in providing goods and services.

It is not surprising that conservatives would fashion their agenda in a way that makes it more palatable to the bulk of the population, most of whom are not wealthy and therefore do not benefit from policies that distribute income upward. However, it is surprising that so many liberals and progressives, who oppose conservative policies, eagerly accept the conservatives' framing of the national debate over economic and social policy. This is comparable to playing a football game where one side gets to determine the defense that the other side will play. This would be a huge advantage in a football game, and it is a huge advantage in politics. As long as liberals allow conservatives to write the script from which liberals argue, they will be at a major disadvantage in policy debates and politics.

The conservative framing of issues is so deeply embedded that it has been widely accepted by ostensibly neutral actors, such as policy professionals or the news media that report on national politics. For example, news reports routinely

---

[1] Of course patent and copyright protection serves a purpose as do all forms of protectionism. They are a mechanism that the government uses to provide incentives for innovation and creative work. However, the relevant question from the standpoint of determining public policy is whether these are the *best* mechanisms for this purpose. It isn't possible to seriously answer this question, unless we first recognize that there are other possible ways to finance innovation and creative work and then to compare the costs and benefits of the various alternative mechanisms.

2

refer to bilateral trade agreements, such as NAFTA or CAFTA, as "free trade" agreements. This is in spite of the fact that one of the main purposes of these agreements is to increase patent protection in developing countries, effectively increasing the length and force of government-imposed monopolies. Whether or not increasing patent protection is desirable policy, it clearly is not "free trade."

It is clever policy for proponents of these agreements to label them as "free trade" agreements (everyone likes freedom), but that is not an excuse for neutral commentators to accept this definition. Back in the 1980s, President Reagan named the controversial MX missile system the "Peacekeeper" to make it more palatable to the public. Thankfully, the media continued to use the neutral "MX" name to describe the missile system. However, when it comes to trade agreements, the media have been every bit as anxious to use the term "peacekeeper" as the proponents of the agreements, using the expression "free trade" almost exclusively to describe these agreements. (In using this term, reporters disregard their normal concern about saving space, since "trade agreement" takes less space than "free-trade agreement.")

In fact, the media have even gone one step further – they routinely denounce the opponents of these trade agreements as "protectionists." This would be like having the *New York Times* refer to the opponents of the MX missile as "warmongers" in a standard news story covering the debate over the new missile. You're doing pretty well in a public debate when you get the media to completely accept your language and framing of issues. It's not easy winning the argument over the MX, when the media and policy experts describe opponents of the missile as "warmongers."

Unfortunately, the state of the current debate on economic policy is even worse from the standpoint of progressives. Not only have the conservatives been successful in getting the media and the experts to accept their framing and language, they have been largely successful in getting their liberal opponents to accept this framing and language, as well. In the case of trade policy, opponents of NAFTA-type trade deals usually have to explain how they would ordinarily support "free trade," but not this particular deal. Virtually no one in the public debate stands up and says that these trade deals have nothing to do with free trade.

Remarkably, the public has enough good sense to recognize that these trade agreements do not in general advance their interests (unless they are in the protected minority), so that NAFTA-type trade deals remain unpopular. If the public voices in the debate would ever stop accepting the conservative framing of the argument, it is very likely that these protectionist pacts could no longer be slipped through Congress. Even with a debate that largely accepts the conservative framing, it is getting increasingly difficult to pass these agreements.

While trade policy has been the topic of many heated public debates in recent years, it is just one of the areas in which the nanny-state conservatives have been able to tilt the framing of the debate to favor their goals. In nearly every important area of economic policy, conservatives have set the terms of debate in ways that make the liberal/progressive opinion unpalatable to the bulk of the population. Unless the debate is reframed in a way that more closely corresponds to reality, conservatives will continue to be successful in their agenda of using government intervention to distribute income upward. This book examines the areas in which the hand of the nanny state is most visible in pushing income to those at the top.

Chapter 1 – Doctors and Dishwashers: How the Nanny State Creates Good Jobs for Those at the Top

The first chapter deals with the most basic issue, how the nanny state ensures that doctors and other highly educated professionals are in short supply, and that the supply of less-skilled workers is relatively plentiful. A big part of this story is trade. The conservative nanny state makes it easy to import goods as a way to replace much of the work done by workers in manufacturing, such as autoworkers, steel workers, and textile workers. Twenty-five years ago, manufacturing was an important source of middle class jobs for workers without college degrees, typically offering health care and pension benefits, in addition to a middle class wage. If goods produced by workers in developing countries (who typically earn only a small fraction of the wages of U.S. workers) can be imported, then the demand for the manufacturing workers in the United States will be reduced, placing downward pressure on the wages and compensation not only of manufacturing workers, but of workers without college degrees in general.

Immigration is another part of the story. The conservative nanny state allows many less-skilled workers into the country to fill jobs at lower wages than employers would be forced to pay the native born population. While allowing immigrant workers into the country can be seen as part of the free market, like allowing imported goods into the country, this is only half of the picture. The conservative nanny state puts on strict controls to limit the extent to which doctors, lawyers, economists, journalists, and other highly paid professionals must face foreign competition. These restrictions take a variety of forms, which will be discussed more thoroughly in Chapter 1, but the key point is that not everyone's labor is placed in international competition. Those at the top of the wage ladder get to enjoy protected labor markets. This both raises their wages and means that everyone else must pay more money for their services.

The conservative nanny state also involves itself in other ways to ensure that highly skilled workers are paid well, and the rest of us pay the taxes in the form of higher prices for the goods and services they produce. For example, licensing requirements, like admission to the bar for lawyers, often are designed more to restrict supply than to ensure quality for consumers.

On the other side, the conservative nanny state beats up on less skilled workers when they push too hard to restrict their supply in the same way. One way the nanny state hampers efforts by less-skilled workers to push up their wages is by outlawing many types of union activity. For example, secondary strikes are illegal. This means that one group of workers can't stage a strike in support of a second group of workers (e.g. truck drivers can't refuse to deliver food to a restaurant where the workers are on strike). In the case of a secondary strike, the conservative nanny state will fine or even imprison workers for being too aggressive in pushing for higher wages. Apparently, employers are too weak to be able to bargain with workers without help from the government.

Of course, this is all supposed to happen behind the scenes, no one is supposed to notice these forms of government intervention. The conservatives want the public to believe that the differences in pay between doctors and dishwashers result from nothing other than the natural workings of the market.

Chapter 2 – The Workers Are Getting Uppity, Call In the Fed!

The second chapter focuses on the Federal Reserve Board, a tremendously important, but little understood government institution. The Fed effectively controls the number of people who have jobs by adjusting its interest rate policy. While it is not always easy to boost the economy by lowering interest rates, the Fed can generally slow the economy and limit employment by raising interest rates.

Higher interest rates reduce home and car buying, and make it more expensive for firms to borrow money to finance new investment. When the Fed perceives inflation as being too great a problem, it raises interest rates to limit employment growth. If it raises interest rates far enough, then it can actually cause the economy to start losing jobs, thereby raising the unemployment rate. A higher unemployment rate puts downward pressure on wages. If wages start to drop, then there is less inflationary pressure in the economy and the Fed has accomplished its goal, although it comes at the cost of higher unemployment and lower wages.

This is not the whole story. The Fed's interest rate hikes do not affect all workers evenly.

When the Fed raises interest rates to slow the economy and increase unemployment, the people who disproportionately lose their jobs are the more disadvantaged groups in society, specifically workers with less education and racial and ethnic minorities. Firms do not lay off their CEOs and top managers when business slows, they lay off assembly line workers, custodians, sales clerks and other workers viewed as disposable. This means workers without college degrees are far more likely to end up unemployed when the Fed raises rates than workers with college or advanced degrees.

Hispanic and African American workers can also expect to take a hit when the Fed cracks down. As a rule of thumb, the unemployment rate for Hispanics is about 1.5 times the overall unemployment rate. For African Americans, the ratio is typically 2 to 1, and for African American teens the ratio is 6 to 1. This means that if the Fed's interest rate hikes raise the overall unemployment rate by 1 percentage point, then they will likely raise the unemployment rate for Hispanics by 1.5 percentage points, for African Americans by 2 percentage points, and for African American teens by 6 percentage points.

The impact on wages follows the impact on employment. The low unemployment years of the late 1990s were the only time in the last quarter century when most workers, including those at the bottom, enjoyed consistent gains in real wages and saw improvements in living standards. Employers complained that they were being forced to accommodate workers' needs for child care and even parental care in the case of some workers with frail parents. The Fed usually stands ready to address employers' concerns about such demands by raising rates, thereby raising unemployment and reducing workers' bargaining power.

There is clearly a need to prevent inflation from spiraling out of control, but how urgent the need is at any point in time is a matter subject to political debate. Since some segments of the population are asked to pay a high price in the form of unemployment and lower wages, they may view the Fed's anti-inflation policy differently than the investors and better-situated workers, who are unlikely to suffer. It may also be worth trying other mechanisms to restrain inflation that distribute the costs differently. (In the old days, governments tried wage-price guidelines and controls.) While there are economic costs associated with other tools aimed at stemming inflation, there are also massive economic costs associated with a Fed policy that deliberately keeps millions of people out of work. The nanny state conservatives don't want the public to even notice that the Fed is making fundamental policy decisions, but in a real debate over economic policy, the truth must come out.

Chapter 3 – The Secret of High CEO Pay and Other Mysteries of the Corporation

Pay for CEOs and other top corporate executives in the United States has soared in recent years, even as the wages of ordinary workers have stagnated. The conventional argument is that CEOs get multi-million dollar salaries because they are highly productive - firms are willing to pay these executives what their services are worth.

This argument is implausible for several reasons. First, today's CEOs don't seem in any obvious way more productive than the CEOs of 30 years ago, who were well compensated, but not nearly as well as today's crop of top executives. Second, CEOs of foreign corporations don't get anywhere near as much compensation. Even the most successful executives in Japan and Europe don't get the ten and hundred million dollar pay packages that are the standard for top executives in the United States. Finally, many of the people who get these seven and eight figure salaries prove incompetent – even when the definition of success is defined narrowly as increasing corporate profits. When top executives walk away in failure they are often given bonuses in the millions of dollars – more than a full lifetime of earnings for a typical worker. In short, there seems little basis for the claim that the pay of top executives reflects their productivity.

The more obvious answer is that the pay of CEOs is determined by corporate boards, many of the members of which are appointed by, or serve at the whim of, the CEOs. Ostensibly, corporate boards are accountable to their shareholders. But with ownership increasingly concentrated among investment funds, whose managers have little time or interest in running individual companies (it is easier to sell the stock than change corporate managers), the CEOs often get free run to do what they want, including giving themselves high pay.

The conservative nanny state plays a big role in allowing high CEO pay, because the corporation is itself a creation of the government. While nanny state conservatives don't like to call attention to this fact, in a free market corporations do not exist. In a free market, individuals can form partnerships and engage in whatever trade and commercial relations they please, but they cannot establish a new legal entity that exists independently of the individuals who own it. Only a government can create a corporation as a legal entity with its own rights and privileges, the most important of which is limited liability.[2]

The privileges of corporate status are clearly valuable to shareholders. We know this because individuals form corporations, even though it means that they have to pay a corporate income tax in addition to the income tax paid by individual shareholders.[3] As a condition of gaining corporate status, the government can and does set rules for corporate governance. (For example, there are extensive rules on the rights of minority shareholders.) Rules of corporate governance could easily include provisions that put a check on runaway CEO pay. For example, it would be relatively simple to require that pay packages be periodically subject to approval by a majority of shareholders, in an election in which only the shares that are actually voted count. (Most corporations count shares that are not voted as supporting the management's position.)

Whether or not such rules on corporate conduct are desirable is a debatable issue, but in a world where the government by definition sets the rules for corporate governance, any set of rules necessarily involves government intervention. The nanny state conservatives would like the public to believe that the current rules of corporate governance were part of the Ten Commandments and should never be altered. In a serious national debate over economic policy, these rules must be part of the discussion.

---

[2] Limited liability means that the shareholders in a corporation cannot be personally held liable for the debts of a corporation. For example, if a factory blows up and destroys the surrounding neighborhood, the people in the area can seize any assets held by the corporation, but if these assets are not enough to compensate for the damage caused, they cannot collect any money from the individual shareholders.

[3] Nanny state conservatives like to describe the corporate income tax as a form of "double taxation" since profit is taxed both at the corporate level and when it is paid out to individual shareholders. In reality, the corporate income tax is a voluntary tax that is a payment to the government in exchange for the privileges granted by corporate status. If shareholders did not feel that the value of these privileges exceeded the tax, then they would restructure corporations as partnerships, which are not subject to a separate income tax.

Chapter 4 – Bill Gates – Welfare Mom: How Government Patent and Copyright Monopolies Enrich the Rich and Distort the Economy

In policy discussions, patents and copyrights are usually treated as part of the natural order, their enforcement is viewed as being as basic as the right to free speech or the free exercise of religion. In fact, there is nothing natural about patents and copyrights, they are relics of the Medieval guild system. They are state-granted monopolies, the exact opposite of a freely competitive market. The nanny state will arrest an entrepreneur who sells a patent-protected product in competition with the person to whom it has granted a patent monopoly.

Patents and copyrights do serve an economic purpose – they are a way to promote research and innovation in the case of patents, and a means of supporting creative and artistic work in the case of copyrights. However, just because patents and copyrights can be used for these purposes, it does not follow that they are the only mechanisms or the most efficient mechanisms to accomplish these purposes.

Both patent and copyright protection have led to increasing inefficiencies and abuses in recent years, exactly the effects that economists would predict from government-granted monopolies. Drug patents have been especially problematic. Because drug companies stand to make such enormous profits from patented drugs, there is a continuous stream of scandals involving efforts to conceal negative research findings, to falsely tout the benefits of specific drugs, and payoffs to experts, regulators, and politicians. In addition, drug patents lead to drugs being priced at levels that make them unaffordable for much of the population in the United States and around the world. While drugs are almost invariably cheap to manufacture, and therefore would sell for a low price in a competitive market, patent monopolies allow drug companies to sell life-saving drugs for thousands or even tens of thousands of dollars per prescription.

Copyrights similarly make items that would otherwise be cheap, or even free over the Internet, very expensive. The cost of transferring recorded music, movies, video games, or software is trivial in the Internet age. However, instead of allowing consumers to benefit from breakthroughs in technology, the entertainment industry has sought to make it illegal to produce certain types of hardware and software, precisely because they facilitate the transfer of material.

Patent and copyright protection also has the effect of making certain companies and individuals very rich. Bill Gates is incredibly rich because the government will imprison anyone who makes copies of Windows without Mr. Gates' permission. Many other rich people have similarly benefited from the government's willingness to prevent free competition. Similarly, huge corporations like Pfizer, Merck, Time-Warner, and the New York Times Company are completely dependent for their profits on the nanny state's protection from competition.

It is necessary to have mechanisms for supporting innovation, and many alternatives to patents and copyrights already exist. The government directly funds $30 billion a year in biomedical research through the National Institutes

8

of Health, a sum that is almost as large as the amount that the pharmaceutical industry claims to spend. A vast amount of creative work is supported by universities and private foundations. While these alternative mechanisms would have to be expanded, or new ones created, in the absence of patent and copyright protection, they demonstrate that patents and copyrights are not essential for supporting innovation and creative work. The appropriate policy debate is whether they are the best mechanisms.

Chapter 5 – Mommy, Joey Owes Me Money: How Bankruptcy Laws are Bailing Out the Rich

True libertarians want to minimize the role of the government in people's lives. If such people exist, they were staunchly opposed to the recent revisions of the bankruptcy laws that make it much more difficult for people to eliminate their debts by declaring bankruptcy.

Part of being a good businessperson is being able to assess a customer's creditworthiness. If a business consistently extends credit to people who can't pay it off, then it is obviously not a good judge of credit risk. In a market economy, such businesses should go out of business, they should not be allowed to run to the government to act as their debt collector. Making the government into a debt collector leads it to become involved far more extensively in people's lives.

Historically, most loans were attached to physical property, such as houses or farms. This made the issue of debt collection relatively simple. If a debtor fell sufficiently behind in repaying a loan, then the creditor simply asked the court to turn over to them the deed for property that provided collateral (a house or a farm). This was a one-time transaction that ended the government's involvement in the case.

However, the new bankruptcy statute gives the courts the responsibility of acting as a debt collector on a continuous basis. The courts must continually monitor the earnings of a debtor who has declared bankruptcy to determine how much money should be turned over to creditors. It must assess factors like their requirements for necessary work-related expenditures (a car, for example), medical care, or for supporting children. Needless to say, this process will bring the government directly into the lives of millions of people. It will also provide a serious disincentive to work for people who have declared bankruptcy, since being forced to pay money to a creditor has the same disincentive effect as being required to pay taxes to the government. For these reasons, people who like to minimize the role of government should support bankruptcy rules that make one-time transfers, thus allowing people to get on with their lives. The International Monetary Fund (IMF) is the international counterpart to the domestic bankruptcy laws. Investors typically get a much higher rate of return on money they invest in developing countries, precisely because there is a higher risk associated with these investments. It is far more likely that the government of Argentina or Russia will default on their bonds than the United States or Germany.

However, the IMF has actively worked to reduce this risk. It regularly threatens countries that consider defaulting on debts or restructuring them in ways that are less favorable to creditors. It seeks to act as an agent of a credit cartel, for both public and private creditors, ensuring that debts in the developing world will be repaid to the greatest extent possible. Just as with domestic bankruptcy laws, those who favor a minimal government would like to see investors held responsible for their own bad investment decisions. If they invest in a country that subsequently defaults on its debt, then this should be the problem of the investor, not a public institution like the IMF.

Nanny state conservatives don't think that businesses can be trusted to make smart lending decisions. They think that businesses need the nanny state to help them collect bad debts, whether from individuals in the United States, or from businesses and governments in other countries.

Chapter 6 – The Rigged Legal Deck: Takings and Torts (The Nanny State Only Gives)

In a market economy, people are supposed to be able to freely contract as they choose. This raises the question of why so many conservatives want the government to ban certain types of contracts. Specifically, "tort reform" laws at both the state and national level limit the type of contingency fees that clients could arrange to pay their attorneys. These laws restrict the percentage of a legal settlement that can be paid to a lawyer and impose other restrictions on the type of contracts that people can sign with lawyers, if they want to sue a corporation.

These restrictions can make a difference in the public's ability to sue large corporations, because many clients do not have money to pay a lawyer in advance. They instead must pay them following any settlement, if they win one. Since there is often a great deal of risk in legal suits (it is difficult to know how a judge or jury will rule), and corporations can make suits extremely costly by filing many motions, the contingent fee (which depends on winning the case) that a lawyer requests may be fairly large.

Libertarians would not object to large contingent fees – if clients don't want to pay them, then they can look for another lawyer. However, the conservatives have promoted caps on contingency fees ostensibly as a way of protecting clients. In reality, such caps are an infringement on individuals' right to freely contract. In a market economy, the government should not be determining which contracts are acceptable for people to sign. But conservatives want the nanny state to make it more difficult to collect damages from big corporations, so they have no problem with this form of governmental intervention in the market.

In recent years, many conservatives have expressed concern about governmental "takings" in which regulations or zoning restrictions (often for environmental purposes) lower the value of a person's property. They have argued that property owners should be compensated for any takings.

There are two important problems with this argument. First, there is a basic asymmetry; the government takes actions all the time. Some of its actions may lower property values, but others raise values. For example, creating a park increases the value of the property near the park. Similarly, building a highway that makes it easier to commute to a major city increases the value of land that can be sold for suburban development. The government doesn't get compensated by private landowners when it increases the value of their land, therefore the payments would be entirely one-sided if the government was forced to compensate landowners when it reduced the value of their property. Of course, this is exactly the sort of nanny state that conservatives want – it only gives them handouts, it never takes anything away.

The second problem with the "takings" argument is that a policy that allows property owners to be compensated every time the government does something to reduce the value of their property would flood the courts with lawsuits. Can someone sue if the government opens an airport ten miles away, shuts a school, or allows a sports stadium to be built in the area? A reasonable conservative argument is that intelligent property owners understand that there is a risk that the government will take actions that will affect the value of property. In principle, this risk is built into the price of the property. If property owners are too dumb to understand the risk when they purchase property, why should the nanny state come to their rescue?

In fact, the traditional legal theory on takings, espoused most clearly by Richard Posner, a conservative legal scholar, is that the government should compensate property owners only in extreme cases where the government's actions amount to a near-total taking of the value of the property (e.g. building a hazardous waste dump on nearby property). This minimizes the role for government, and encourages property owners to be mindful of potential risks before they buy property.

Chapter 7 — Small Business Babies

Entrepreneurs do not have to pass competence tests or get government approval for their business plan before opening a small business. This is as it should be. However, it means that many people, who have no idea what they are doing, start businesses with business plans that cannot possibly succeed. It is, therefore, not surprising that most small businesses close after just a few years; that is the way a market economy works.

However, small businesses have a privileged place in conservative ideology. Conservatives shower them with tax breaks, low interest loans, and exemptions from a wide variety of regulations covering everything from workplace health and safety to environmental concerns. As a practical matter, it is not always clear what public interest is served by preferential treatment for small businesses. For example, it is not clear why it would be desirable for workers at small businesses to have weaker workplace safety protections than workers at larger companies. It is also not clear why the public should subsidize small businesses with special tax breaks, some of which may in fact just be subsidies for the personal consumption of small business owners. (The tax deduction that many small business owners take on company cars often are just subsidies for their family car.)

Small businesses can provide a valuable service for larger corporations – they can provide a pleasant face that advances their interests. Large corporations will often make public arguments against rules that affect them negatively by arguing that the rules will hurt small businesses. This argument has been especially effective with minimum wage laws. While higher minimum wages may hurt the profits of small businesses, the biggest losers are typically large corporations, like McDonald's, that employ many low-wage earners. It is very helpful to these companies to hide behind the small businesses that could get hurt by higher minimum wages.

Another example is the effort to abolish the estate tax. Proponents of repeal have routinely argued that the tax causes many families to lose their businesses. In reality, almost by definition, small business owners will not owe any estate tax – their estate will be too small. Yet tens of millions of people support repealing the estate tax because they are worried about the effect it has on family businesses.

Because small businesses serve this important political purpose, and small business owners are a largely conservative constituency, nanny state conservatives will continue to shower government largesse on small businesses. And then they will insist that we should leave everything to the market.

Chapter 8 – Taxes: It's Not Your Money

Conservatives have often used the refrain "It's your money" in reference to the money that taxpayers owe to the government. This refrain is used to justify various tax dodges, including outright evasion. In fact, once the tax laws have been set, the money that people owe the government is not "their" money, it belongs to the government. In this way, tax liabilities are like the condominium fees that individual units are assessed. This is money owed to the condominium association, it does not belong to the owner of the individual condominium.

The nanny state conservatives want the country's tax cheats to be treated with kid gloves. Most of the serious tax cheats are relatively wealthy (this is true almost by definition – poor people don't owe much money in taxes). While most nanny state conservatives are anxious to throw the book at a welfare recipient who gets $1,000-$2,000 more than what she is entitled to, they would coddle tax cheats who owe the government tens or even hundreds of thousands of dollars. One can argue about how the tax law should be structured and what rates should be set, but the fact that there are disagreements on these issues does not mean that the tax laws should not be enforced.

It is important to remember that there is no free lunch in this story. The government needs a certain amount of money to pay its bills. If it gets less from one person, then it has to get more from everyone else. It's very nice to give people a tax break on the money they make from selling their home or to lower the tax rate on capital gains or dividends, but these tax breaks mean that taxes must be higher on the people who don't benefit from them, since the government still needs the same amount of money. Coincidentally, conservatives tend to argue that people should not pay taxes on the types of income that most rich people get (capital gains and dividends). They would rather have all taxes be paid out of wage income, which happens to be the major source of income for most low- and middle-income people in the country.

Chapter 9 – Don't Make Big Business Compete Against Government Bureaucrats

While the nanny state conservatives ostensibly want to limit the role of government, there are some areas in which they acknowledge that government can provide services more efficiently and effectively, most obviously policing and national defense. Of course, even these services could be provided through the private sector, albeit far less efficiently. People could contract with the policing or defense corporation of their choosing, which would protect them in the manner they view as most appropriate.

Just as the government is the most efficient provider of policing and national defense, it is often the most efficient provider of other social and administrative services. There are sectors where the advantages of a single centralized system can lead to large economies of scale. In such cases, it is more efficient to have a service (e.g. Medicare and Social Security) provided by the government, instead of having a large number of competing firms.

It is not always clear whether the government will be a more efficient provider of a service than the private sector. In some cases this determination can be left to the market, albeit not with policing, national defense, or Social Security. This is happening at the moment with Medicare, where beneficiaries have the option to stay with the government-managed system or to sign up with private insurers. (The vast majority of beneficiaries opt for the government-run system, even though the government subsidizes private insurers in the program.)

In principle, the government could offer the option in other sectors. For example, it can expand the Medicare program and let every person or employer in the country buy into it on a voluntary basis. Similarly, it could establish a nationwide voluntary pension system (with both defined benefit and defined contribution options) as an add-on to Social Security. Individuals and employers that prefer the public system to the options available from the private sector would have the option to contribute to this system. Those who prefer private sector pension plans and savings vehicles could stay with their existing plans.

The conventional view among conservatives is that the private sector is lean and mean, full of innovative and efficient businesses. By contrast, the government is composed of lazy and wooly-headed bureaucrats who couldn't make it in the business world (or they would be there). Given this view, they should have little concern about the prospect of having private businesses compete with the government. If the conservative view of the greater efficiency of the private sector is right, then it should quickly defeat any competitor sponsored by the government.

In reality, it is striking how worried private businesses often get over the prospect of competing with the government. For example, when Congress was debating a Medicare prescription drug benefit in 2003, private insurers (and the pharmaceutical industry) insisted that Medicare not be allowed to directly offer its own insurance program for prescription drugs. They got this prohibition written into the law.

Back in the late 1990s, several express mail companies actually went into court to try to force the U.S. Postal Service to abandon an ad campaign that was proving very effective. The Postal Service ads pointed that its express mail service was much cheaper than FedEx or UPS. After the courts refused to outlaw the ad campaign, the express mail companies went to their friends in Congress, who effectively tamed the competition.

It benefits the economy as a whole to have these services provided in the most efficient way. Of course, the firms that stand to profit by providing these services do not care about inefficiency, they care about their profits. And this means that they do whatever is necessary to ensure that they never have to compete against the government.

Conclusion – Beyond the Conservative Nanny State

The idea that conservatives trust the market while progressives want the government is a myth. Conservatives simply are not honest about the ways in which they want the government to intervene to distribute income upwards. Once this myth is exposed, it allows for a whole different framing of a wide range of policy issues. We can recognize that both conservatives and liberals favor a wide variety of government interventions in the economy – and also want many decisions left to the market. This view can allow us to look at a wide range of policies from a different angle.

In trade policy, we can decide which areas should be placed in competition, and how. At the moment, the nanny state conservatives are the biggest protectionists around. If we want workers in the United States to compete directly with workers in the developing world, then it probably makes the most sense to start at the top. Trade policy should focus on putting our doctors, lawyers, and economists in competition with professionals in the developing world, not our least-skilled workers. This strategy offers the greatest opportunity for economic gain, in addition to distributing income downward.

Regarding Federal Reserve Board policy, we may consider other ways than high unemployment to ensure that inflation remains tame. And, we may be willing to take more risks with inflation than the nanny state conservatives want.

Corporations are an effective governmental tool to facilitate economic growth and the accumulation of wealth. The government certainly has the prerogative to set rules that limit the ability of high-level corporate executives to pilfer from the corporation. Remember, no one is forced to form a corporation.

There are many ways to support innovative and creative work. There is no reason to believe that patents and copyrights (or any other relics from the Middle Ages) are the most efficient mechanisms in a 21st century economy.

In a free market, the government does not act as an all-purpose debt collector. Creditors must be taught that they are taking risks and they cannot count on the government to bail them out.

In a free market, people must be allowed to collect damages from those who have harmed them. Reforms to the legal system that make this process more efficient are desirable. The public has no reason to support changes in rules that stack the deck in favor of big corporations so that it is more difficult for those who have been harmed to win compensation.

Most small business owners are honest, hardworking people, just like most other people who work for a living. The government has no special obligations to small business owners, many of whom will inevitably lose money and go out of business.

Finally, there are many areas in which the government can provide services more efficiently than the private sector. There is no reason to apologize for providing a service in the most efficient way. If private businesses can't compete with the government, it is their problem.

Exposing the truth of the conservative nanny state opens up a whole new range of policy options, only a fraction of which will be discussed in this book. However, it should be clear that if progressives ever want to start winning national debates on economic policy we must stop using scripts that were written by conservatives. The market can be a fantastic force for promoting economic growth and allowing an arena for individual freedom, but it exists in a structure set out by the government. If we cannot question the structure established by the nanny state conservatives, then we are not really debating the policies that determine the well-being of hundreds of millions of people in the United States and around the world. We're just putting on a show.

CHAPTER ONE

Doctors and Dishwashers

How the Nanny State Creates Good Jobs for Those at the Top

From 1980 to 2005 the economy grew by more than 120 percent. Productivity, the amount of goods and services produced in an average hour of work, rose by almost 70 percent. Yet the wage for a typical worker changed little over this period, after adjusting for inflation. Furthermore, workers had far less security at the end of this period than the beginning, as access to health insurance and pension coverage dwindled, and layoffs and downsizing became standard practices. In short, most workers saw few gains from a quarter century of economic growth.

But the last 25 years have not been bad news for everyone. Workers with college degrees, and especially workers with advanced degrees like doctors, lawyers, and accountants, have fared quite well over this period. These workers have experienced large gains in wages and living standards since 1980. The wage for a worker at the cutoff for the top 5 percent of wage-earners rose by more than 40 percent between 1980 and 2001. Those at the cutoff for the top 1.0 percent saw their wages increase by almost 75 percent over this period.[1] The average doctor in the country now earns more than $180,000 a year.[2] A minimum wage earner has to put in 2 days of work to pay for an hour of his doctor's time. (After adding in the overhead fees for operating the doctor's office, the minimum wage earner would have to work even longer.)

While doctors, lawyers, and accountants don't pull down the same money as corporate CEOs or the Bill Gates types, their success is hugely important in sustaining the conservative nanny state. If the only people doing well in the current economy were a tiny strata of super-rich corporate heads and high-tech entrepreneurs, there would be little political support for sustaining the system. Since the list of winners also includes the most educated segment of society, it creates a much more sustainable system. In addition to being a much broader segment of the population (5-10 percent as opposed to 0.5 percent), this group of highly educated workers includes the people who write news stories and editorial columns, teach college classes, and shape much of what passes for political debate in the country. The fact that these people benefit from the conservative nanny state vastly strengthens its hold.

---

[1] These data can be found in Dew-Becker and Gordon (2005, Table 8).
[2] Data on doctors' salaries (net of malpractice insurance) can be found in Lowes (2005).

The Basic Conservative Nanny State Mythology

This larger group of professionals has constructed and promoted the key myth of the conservative nanny state; they have succeeded where others have failed because they have the ability and education to succeed in the 21st century world economy. The problem with the others that have fallen behind – the autoworkers, the shop clerks, the restaurant workers etc. – is that they don't have the skills needed to compete. The remedy of the nanny state conservatives is to either tell the losers to be more like them and work harder (the Republican nanny state conservatives) or express sympathy and throw a few dollars at vocational education and trade adjustment assistance (the Democratic nanny state conservatives). The key to a real solution is to move beyond the conservative nanny state mythology.

It doesn't take sophisticated economics to understand how some professionals have fared well in recent decades, even as most workers have done poorly; it is a simple story of supply and demand. The rules of the nanny state are structured to increase the supply of less-skilled labor, while restricting the supply of some types of highly skilled professionals. With more supply, wages fall – the situation of less-skilled workers. With less supply, wages rise – the situation of highly skilled professionals.

While there are many mechanisms through which the nanny state conservatives have increased the supply of less-skilled labor, probably the most visible is trade. Trade agreements that facilitate imports of cars, steel, clothes, and other manufactured goods disproportionately displace less-skilled workers from what had formerly been middle-class jobs with good wages and benefits. Nanny state conservatives usually treat this job loss as an unfortunate byproduct of trade agreements like NAFTA and CAFTA. In fact, the job loss and downward pressure on wages from these agreements are not unfortunate side effects of these trade deals – they are precisely the point of these trade deals.

In economic theory, the gains from trade stem from getting imported goods or services at lower prices. The gains that economists predict from NAFTA and CAFTA stem from getting less-skilled labor (largely the labor of manufacturing workers) in developing countries at a lower price than would have to be paid in the United States. These agreements are explicitly designed to place manufacturing workers in the United States in direct competition with low wage workers in Mexico, Central America, Malaysia, and China. To ensure this outcome, the executives at U.S. corporations are asked directly what laws and trade restrictions prevent them from investing in developing countries and taking advantage of their low-wage labor.

Whatever obstacles exist to foreign investment are removed through these trade pacts. This means not only the elimination of tariff barriers or quotas that directly restrict imports from developing countries; these trade deals also place restrictions on the types of health and safety regulations that can be imposed in the United States. These restrictions ensure that health and safety regulations do not obstruct imports from developing countries, thereby acting as barriers to trade. The trade deals also restrict the ability of developing countries to tax or control the profits of foreign investors, thereby providing much greater security to corporations planning to build factories in developing countries. In short, these trade deals are designed to make sure that an autoworker in Detroit has to compete head to head with an autoworker in China, and that anything obstructing this competition is removed.

This may look like free trade, but it is only half the picture. The trade pacts have done little or nothing to remove the extensive licensing and professional barriers that prevent foreign doctors, lawyers, economists, and journalists from competing on an equal footing with their counterparts in the United States. While the corporate CEOs are invited into the planning sessions, if not the actual negotiations, to ensure that barriers to competition with Chinese autoworkers are eliminated, there is no comparable effort to ensure that barriers to Indian doctors, lawyers, accountants, etc., are eliminated.

If U.S. trade negotiators approached the highly paid professions in the same way they approached the auto industry, then they would actively be trying to uncover all the factors that prevent direct competition between U.S. professionals and their counterparts in the developing world, and then construct trade agreements that eliminated these barriers. They would be asking hospitals, law firms, and universities what is preventing them from doubling, tripling, or quadrupling the number of doctors, lawyers, and economists from developing countries working in their institutions. They would also be asking the trade negotiators from Mexico, India, or China what obstacles prevent them from sending hundreds of thousands of highly skilled professionals to the United States.

This does not happen. In fact, the exact opposite happens. In 1997 Congress tightened the licensing rules for foreign doctors entering the country because of concerns by the American Medical Association and other doctors' organizations that the inflow of foreign doctors was driving down their salaries. As a result, the number of foreign medical residents allowed to enter the country each year was cut in half. [3]

For some reason, the editorial boards, political pundits, and trade economists managed to completely ignore this protectionist measure, even though its impact dwarfed the impact of most of the "free trade" trade agreements that they have promoted so vigorously. If free trade in physicians brought doctors' salaries down to European levels, the savings would be close to $100,000 per doctor, approximately $80 billion a year. This is 10 times as large as standard estimates of the gains from NAFTA.

---

[3] For a discussion of the debate over the impact of foreign doctors on the wages of U.S. physicians, see "Caught in the Middle," *Washington Post*, March 19, 1996, "A.M.A. and Colleges Assert There is a Surfeit of Doctors," *New York Times*, March 1, 1997, and "U.S. to Pay Hospitals Not to Train Doctors, Easing Glut," *New York Times*, February 15, 1997. The success of the 1997 policy changes in restricting the inflow of foreign doctors was noted five years later. See "Fewer Foreign Doctors Seek U.S. Training," *Washington Post*, September 4, 2002, and "Test Tied to Slip in Foreign Applicants for Medical Residences," *New York Times*, September 4, 2002.

Most people probably do not realize that the protectionist barriers that keep out foreign professionals are actually quite extensive.[4] This is in part due to efforts by proponents of the conservative nanny state to conceal the protectionist barriers that benefit professionals like themselves. When confronted on the issue, nanny state conservatives are likely to refer to Indian doctors or Chinese scientists they know as evidence that barriers to foreign professionals working in the United States do not exist.

This argument deserves a good laugh and a healthy dose of ridicule. Anyone who tried to claim that the United States did not have protection on apparel because clothing stores sold blue jeans made in Bangladesh would be laughed out of a discussion. Similarly, anyone who claimed that the United States doesn't protect agriculture because it's possible to buy Mexican avocados in the grocery store would be dismissed as a fool. Yet, the world's leading trade economists think that they have shown that there is no protection for economists in the United States because one of their colleagues is from Brazil, or that there is no protection for doctors because they go to an Indian doctor for their check-ups.

If there were no protection for doctors and other professionals in the United States, then smart kids growing up in Beijing or Bombay would have the same likelihood of working as doctors in the United States as smart kids growing up on Long Island. This is not the case because of a wide variety of barriers deliberately constructed to prevent U.S. professionals from being subject to foreign competition.

The most important set of barriers is state specific licensing, which involves distinct and idiosyncratic rules for working in professions like medicine, dentistry, and law. If the United States were committed to free trade in high-paying professions, it would negotiate trade agreements that established international standards in these professions. These standards would be based on recognized health and quality standards, as is the case for consumer safety regulations on manufacturing goods under the WTO. The U.S. standards could be higher than those in developing countries or other rich countries, if we chose, but they would be fully transparent. For example, there would be standardized tests for being licensed, which could be administered anywhere in the world. Furthermore, anyone who met these standards would be able to practice their profession in the United States, regardless of which country they came from. This means that an Indian doctor could train at a licensed medical school in India, take a licensing test in India, and then apply for a job in the United States, where he or she could work for whatever salary they negotiated with their employer.

These sorts of professional licensing rules would allow students to follow professional tracks in any country in the world, knowing that if they did well they would be able to work in their profession in the United States. Such rules would also provide schools and universities in the developing world with the

---

[4] For a partial list of these barriers see Freeman (2003).

incentive to set up training programs explicitly designed to educate professionals to work in the United States.

Just as no one will build a factory in China to export steel to the United States until they know that they will not be obstructed by tariff or quota barriers, no one will design a university curriculum around training students to work as professionals in the United States unless they know that their graduates will have this opportunity. While there would undoubtedly be an immediate surge in foreign professionals entering the United States if barriers were removed, the full effect would only be felt through time as universities in other countries oriented their education toward producing professionals for the U.S. market.

The potential gains from this sort of free trade are enormous. Doctors in the United States earn an average of more than $180,000 a year. Their counterparts in Europe earn less than $80,000 a year.[5] Doctors in the developing world earn considerably less. If enough doctors can be brought in from the developing world to bring doctors' pay down to the European level, the savings to consumers would be $80 billion a year, about $700 per family per year. (It is easy to ensure that the developing world benefits as well – this will be discussed below.) This is the gain from allowing free trade in just one profession. The gains could be many times as large if free trade existed in all of the high paying professions and/or the pay of U.S. professionals was brought in line with that of professionals in the developing world.

It is not only licensing barriers that prevent free trade in professional services. Immigration laws also prevent foreign professionals from competing on an equal footing with professionals in the United States. While it is often possible for a university or other institution to hire a foreign professional under current law, that is, by claiming that no qualified U.S. citizens or permanent residents are available, this is still very far from introducing full-fledged free trade. If there were real free trade in the area of university professors, then it should be as easy for Harvard to hire professors from China as it is for Wal-Mart to import shirts from China.

And, if Harvard does not want to import professors from China (because it's Harvard), then other more entrepreneurial universities would have this opportunity. Since these new Wal-Mart Universities (which could have the same sort of teaching standards and faculty publication requirements as existing universities) could hire faculty of comparable quality to the faculty at existing universities, at a fraction of the price, they could hugely undercut existing universities' tuition. This would force existing universities to either go out of business or adopt similar hiring policies. While university faculty would end up

---

[5] The OECD reports that the average annual pre-tax income of doctors in the United States in 1995 was $196,000. By comparison, it reports that doctors in Switzerland earned an average $82,000, in Japan $57,300, and in Denmark $52,600 (Organization of Economic Cooperation and Development: Development Center. *OECD Health Data, 1998*. Paris: OECD, 1998). While these figures are now somewhat dated, there is no reason to believe that the relative wages have changed.

with lower pay (especially their "free trade" economists), the gains to the public in the form of lower college tuition could be enormous.

In the same vein, the *Wal-Mart Times* and the *Wal-Mart Post* could quickly displace newspapers that pay high salaries to reporters and columnists. There is certainly no shortage of very smart people in India and elsewhere in the developing world who could do outstanding work as journalists and reporters in the United States. As is the case with university faculty, most will never be given the opportunity because they are not allowed to compete on an equal footing with their U.S. born counterparts. If we really had free trade in news reporting, then newspapers in the United States could hire foreign reporters at a fraction of the wage that they currently pay to U.S.- born reporters. The newspapers that adhered to their old pay scales would likely soon find themselves undercut by the competition. The globalized newspapers would be able to charge lower subscription prices and advertising rates, thereby putting the traditional newspapers at a huge disadvantage.

It is important to recognize that reducing the wages of highly paid professionals is not just a matter of beating up on the people who are on top. This is a source of real gains and greater efficiency for the economy as a whole. The high wages received by professionals end up as part of the cost in a wide range of goods and services. The high pay scale of doctors in the United States is one of the main reasons that U.S. health care costs are so much higher than in the rest of the world. (Not all doctors earn exorbitant salaries. Highly paid specialists earn several times the salary of family practitioners.) High salaries for at least some U.S. academics get translated into soaring college tuition. And the high pay received by lawyers, accountants, reporters, and journalists get passed on as expenses that raise the price of a broad set of goods and services. By using trade to reduce the salaries of these highly paid professionals, we would be allowing large increases in living standards for most of the population, and increasing the efficiency of the economy by making professionals in the United States compete on an even footing with professionals elsewhere in the world.

Nanny state conservatives sometimes express concern about the prospect of professionals from developing countries coming to the United States because they claim it amounts to a "brain drain" from developing countries.[6] In fact, it is easy to design policies that ensure that developing countries share in the gains from free trade in professions, as anyone familiar with trade economics should know. To do this, it is only necessary to impose a modest tax (e.g. 10 percent) on the wages of developing country professionals working in the United States, which would be repatriated to their home country as compensation for their training. This tax could be set at a level that far exceeds the actual cost of training so that developing countries could then train two or three doctors, or other professionals, for every one that went to work in the United States.

Such a tax should be relatively simple to enforce; university professors, reporters, doctors, and lawyers are not generally going to be working under the table, so it should not be hard to tax them at their work place. (Professionals

[6] See "Stealing From the Poor to Care for the Rich," *New York Times*, December 14, 2005.

like doctors and lawyers are actually licensed by the government, so proof of payment of the tax could be linked to their license renewal.) Given the huge gap in compensation levels between professionals in developing countries and professionals in the United States, a modest tax would not deter many workers from trying to find jobs in the United States. In addition, developing countries would also benefit from the money that professionals working in the United States would repatriate to family members in their home countries. Given the huge gap in living standards, even a small portion of the wages earned in the United States could have a substantial impact on the economy of a developing country.

Of course, the United States and developing countries will not see these benefits as long as the nanny state conservatives continue to insist on protectionist trade policies. While it is hard to defend these protectionist policies on economic or moral grounds, the nanny state conservatives routinely deny that protection for highly paid professionals exists. It is obviously self-serving to attribute their relative success to their skill and hard-work as opposed to their control over trade policy, but as long as the nanny state conservatives write the news stories and teach the economics courses it will be difficult to get free trade for professionals on the agenda.

Immigration: Another Tool for Wage Depression

Trade is not the only mechanism that nanny state conservatives have used to depress the wages of the bulk of the population. Immigration has also been an important tool to depress the wages of a substantial segment of the workforce. The principle with immigration is exactly the same as with trade. It takes advantage of the billions of workers in developing countries who are willing to work at substantially lower wages than workers in the United States to drive down the wages in a wide range of occupations.

The conservative nanny state folklore on immigration is that immigrants take jobs that workers in the United States do not want, and they point to jobs like custodians, dishwashers, and fruit picking, all very low paying jobs. The problem with the folklore is that the reason that native born workers are unlikely to want these jobs is that they are low-paying, not because they are intrinsically such awful jobs. Native-born workers have been willing to take many unpleasant jobs when they were compensated with high wages. Meatpacking is an obvious example of an industry that did offer relatively high-paying jobs that were widely sought after by native-born workers, even though no one would be very happy to work in a slaughterhouse. This is less true today than in the past, because the meatpacking industry has taken advantage of the availability of immigrant workers to depress wages and working conditions in the industry. As a result, immigrant workers are now a very large share of the workforce in the meatpacking industry.[7]

---

[7] For a discussion of the transformation in the meatpacking industry see Stull, D., M. Broadway, and K. Erickson, 1992. "The Price of a Good Steak: Beef Packing and Its Consequences for

The same sort of situation holds in all of the jobs that native born workers supposedly do not want. Native-born workers will wash dishes, clean toilets, and pick tomatoes for $20 an hour. When the nanny state conservatives say that they can't find native-born workers for these jobs, they mean that they can't find native-born workers at the wages that they want to pay, just as most of us can't find native-born doctors or lawyers who are willing to work for $15 an hour. The difference is that the nanny state conservatives get to bring in immigrants at low wages to meet their needs, whereas the doctors and lawyers can count on the nanny state to protect them from competition with immigrant workers.

The immigration laws end up being an effective conservative nanny state tool in this respect. The current laws do put limits on the numbers of immigrants who can enter the country each year, which should limit the extent to which immigrant workers can place downward pressure on the wages of native born workers. However, a large number of immigrants work in violation of these laws, but overwhelmingly in jobs held by less educated workers (e.g. dishwashers, custodians, fruit pickers).

There are two reasons that this is the case. The first is that less-skilled workers in developing countries have less to risk by working illegally in the United States than more highly skilled workers. In other words, if a person is working in a relatively low-paying job in Mexico or Central America, they are not giving up a lot to work without proper documentation in the United States. On the other hand, doctors, lawyers, or accountants in Mexico or Central America would be risking a relatively secure position in their home countries if they went to the United States with the intention of working illegally. If they got caught and deported, they would be much worse off than if they had stayed in their home country. For this reason, less-skilled workers will be far more likely to risk working illegally in the United States.

On the other side, there are no organized groups in the United States with substantial political power to raise issues about the lack of enforcement of immigration laws when the people being hired are less-skilled workers. If a hospital made a practice of hiring foreign doctors who are in the United States illegally, and paying them a fraction of the prevailing wage for doctors, or a university sought to hire large numbers of immigrant professors who were not legally authorized to work in the United States, it is virtually certain that there would be loud demands from doctors' lobbies and organizations of university faculty, demanding that the laws be enforced.

The result of this situation is that there are a substantial number of people in the developing world who are prepared to come to the United States and work in less-skilled jobs, in violation of U.S. immigration laws. This typically means overstaying a tourist visa, but it can also mean a risky illegal crossing at the border. For employers, this inflow of immigrants means a cheap labor pool that lowers wages in a wide range of less-skilled jobs.

Garden City, Kansas," in *Structuring Diversity: Ethnographic Perspectives on the New Immigration*, ed. L. Lamphere, Chicago, IL: University of Chicago Press.

By contrast, the inflow of more skilled immigrants is restricted largely to those who work in the country legally. The pool of higher-skilled immigrants has been expanded somewhat in recent years with special visa programs, such as the H1-B program, which allows workers with special skills that are deemed to be in short supply (i.e. employers want to pay less) to work in the United States for a limited period of time. However, the supply of higher-skilled immigrants is still dwarfed by the inflow of less-skilled immigrants. In 2005, approximately 190,000 workers were employed on H1-B visas. By contrast, the Census Bureau estimates that more than 5 million immigrants entered the country over the prior decade without legal authorization, the vast majority of these people presumably came to work in less-skilled jobs.

Since there has been a large increase in wages for more educated workers over the last quarter century, and a relative decrease in the wages of less-educated workers, there should be an increase in the inflow of high-skilled workers other things being equal. However, since immigration policy has been deliberately skewed to benefit higher paid workers, it amplifies other factors placing downward pressure on the wages of less skilled workers.

Licensing Requirements and Unions

Trade and immigration are not the only tools that the nanny state conservatives use to ensure a plentiful supply of less skilled labor and a relatively limited supply of more highly skilled labor. They also rely on government licensing requirements to limit the number of people who can work as doctors, lawyers, and in other professions requiring substantial education and/or training. Government licensing means that the nanny state arrests anyone who competes without the appropriate permit.

Licensing requirements do have a legitimate function: they can be a way to ensure quality. When we go to a doctor, we want to know that the person we see is more likely to make us well than to make us sicker. But the actual practice of issuing and controlling licenses is generally designed more to restrict the number of doctors, lawyers, architects, etc., than to ensure the quality of the services these people provide.[8] Perhaps the most obvious way to recognize this fact is that the professional organizations themselves usually have a large amount of control over the number of people who are licensed into a profession in a state. If an association of dishwashers or custodians got to decide the number of people who could legally work as dishwashers or custodians, it is likely that the wages in these occupations would rise considerably. (It is worth remembering that the United States still generally has state specific licensing requirements for professionals. The "free-trade" crew want to have a single set of standards for all forms of merchandise traded all

---

[8] The way in which licensing restricts supply and drives up wages is discussed in Kleiner, M. 2006. *Licensing Occupations: Ensuring Quality or Restricting Competition?*, Kalamazoo, MI: Upjohn Institute for Employment Research.

over the world, but it has apparently escaped their attention that a lawyer from New York can't practice across the river in New Jersey.)

While the conservative nanny state will bring in the cops to make sure that doctors, lawyers, and other highly educated professionals don't face too much competition, it also brings in the cops to ensure that dishwashers and custodians *do* face substantial competition to keep down their wages. This issue comes up most directly with regard to the actions of unions, a mechanism through which some less educated workers have tried to restrict their supply, and thereby put upward pressure on wages.

The conservative nanny state puts very tight restrictions on what it allows unions to do. For example, many types of strikes are illegal. The bosses can have the police arrest strikers, and especially their leaders, for attempting to restrict labor supply in ways not approved by the conservative nanny state. The most obvious way in which this nanny state intervention puts workers at a serious disadvantage is with secondary strikes. This is when one group of workers refuses to perform their job in support of other workers who are on strike.

Secondary strikes can in principle be a very powerful tool for union workers. For example, if truck drivers honor the picket line of striking dishwashers at a restaurant, or striking custodians at a hotel, and refuse to deliver supplies, then the strike will be far more painful for the business owner. This is especially the case in the current economic environment, where it is a standard practice for businesses to simply hire replacement workers when their regular employees go out on strike. If the business is unable to get necessary supplies because truck drivers are honoring a picket line, then replacement workers may not be of much help. The fact that secondary strikes can be so effective is undoubtedly why the conservative nanny state makes them illegal. If doctors or lawyers need help to restrict their supply, then the conservative nanny state is there to answer the call. In the same vein, when those further down the wage ladder try to take actions to restrict the supply of their labor and push up their own wages, the conservative nanny state comes down hard on the other side. There is a clear principle at work here – the conservative nanny state is there to redistribute income upwards.

Are the Free Traders Ready for Free Trade?

The trade agreements that the United States has negotiated over the last three decades have been about getting low cost auto workers, steel workers, and textile workers. In addition, immigration policy has been designed to ensure that custodians, farmworkers, and dishwashers all work for low wages. These policies have been successful in pushing down wages for large segments of the work force, not only those who were directly displaced by trade or immigrant workers, but also those who face heightened competition from workers who were displaced by trade or immigration.

But trade does not have to depress the wages of less-skilled workers. Trade agreements can also be structured to get us low cost doctors, lawyers, accountants, economists, reporters, and editorial writers. There are tens of millions of smart and energetic people in the developing world who could do these jobs better than most of the people who currently hold these positions in the United States. And they would be willing to do these jobs for a fraction of the wage. Real free traders would be jumping at this opportunity to increase economic growth and aid consumers in the United States, while at the same time increasing prosperity in developing countries.

But the economists, editorialists, and political pundits are not likely to raise the call for eliminating the barriers that prevent competition from professionals in the developing world. The truth is that the "free traders" don't want free trade – they want cheap nannies – but "free trade" sounds much more noble.

CHAPTER TWO

The Workers Are Getting Uppity

Call In the Fed!

Much of the conservative nanny state's economic policy is devoted to the principle of keeping doctors and other highly educated professionals in short supply, while at the same time keeping the supply of less-skilled workers plentiful. The Federal Reserve Board is one of the key nanny state tools for maintaining this imbalance. For this reason, it could have been included as a section in the last chapter. But the Fed, with its celebrity former chairman, the Maestro Alan Greenspan, is so important in this story that it deserves its own chapter.

The Federal Reserve Board: What it Does and Who Does It

Alan Greenspan had risen to rock star status by the end of his long reign as Federal Reserve Board chairman, but it is unlikely that most people had any clear idea of what he did. That is how the nanny state conservatives wanted it. While they are no doubt pleased that the public celebrate Mr. Greenspan for his wise management of the economy, when it comes to the details of Fed policy, they prefer to hang a "keep out" sign to avoid potentially unpleasant questions.

The Fed has a more direct effect on the state of the economy than any other institution in the country. At any given time, its policies have the greatest impact on the unemployment rate and the rate of wage growth. For this reason, the public should know how the Fed is making its decisions, and who exactly is calling the shots.

At the most basic level, the Fed controls the short-term interest rate that banks charge each other to lend money overnight to meet their legal reserve requirements.[1] This interest rate – the federal funds rate – is a key rate because it is the basis for other short term interest rates. If the Fed raises the federal funds rate, it will lead banks to raise the interest rates they charge on short-term loans to businesses or families.

This has the effect of discouraging borrowing and reducing the buying power of those who do borrow, since they now must pay higher interest on their loans. For example, if a business can get a 3-month loan at a 4 percent interest rate it may decide to borrow money to expand its inventory. On the other hand, if the interest rate is 5 percent, the business may decide not to expand its inventory. Families may make the same sort of decision about buying a new car. If they can get a car loan at 4 percent interest, they may choose to

---

[1] It also has a number of other important responsibilities involving the regulation and oversight of the country's financial system. This discussion will focus on the Fed's control of interest rates because it relates most directly to the focus of the book, but its regulatory role is also extremely important and can also have substantial distributional consequences.

buy a new car. On the other hand, at 5 percent, they may decide to live with their old car for a while longer.

Now that many loans have adjustable interest rates, raising the short-term rate can cause the rate for adjustable car loans or mortgages to rise. For example, if a person bought a car with a loan set at a 4 percent interest rate, and then the federal funds rate went up by 2 percentage points, she might find that the interest rate on her loan is now 6 percent.[2] The same thing would happen to people who have adjustable rate mortgages. They would see the interest rate on their mortgage rise, thereby increasing their monthly mortgage payment, leaving less money for other expenses.

The effect of interest rates is even more important when higher short-term interest rates lead to an increase in long-term interest rates, most importantly traditional 15- or 30-year fixed rate mortgages. Long-term interest rates don't always follow short-term interest rates, but if short-term rates rise by a large amount, long-term interest rates, such as mortgage rates, will usually rise as well. Long-term interest rates are important for the economy because they affect home construction and home buying, and also affect the ability of people to borrow against their homes for other expenses. In addition, long-term interest rates affect the ability of firms to borrow to finance new investment.

Through these various channels, higher interest rates reduce demand in the economy, slowing growth and job creation. This is the incredible power of the Fed. When it wants to slam the brakes on the economy, it raises interest rates. Higher interest rates effectively prevent the economy from growing, and keep workers from getting jobs.

The Fed can also help to speed growth by lowering interest rates, thereby encouraging borrowing and investing. As a general rule, it is easier to slow growth by raising interest rates than speed growth by lowering rates. At high enough interest rates consumers will cut back on car buying, home buying, and other purchases, and companies will delay their investment plans. While lower interest rates encourage growth, by themselves they are not always sufficient to get an economy back on track when it falls into a recession, as Japan discovered in the nineties.[3] In an economy where workers fear losing their jobs, few people will buy new cars or take on unnecessary debt regardless of how low interest rates go. Also, even at low rates firms will not invest if they don't see demand for their products.

---

[2] Interest rates generally don't all change by exactly the same amount, but they do tend to move in the same direction. For example, if the federal funds rate rises by 2 percentage points, then the interest rate on a car loan will probably increase, but most likely by somewhat less than 2 percentage points.

[3] After the collapse of its stock and real estate bubbles at the beginning of the nineties, Japan's economy entered a period of prolonged stagnation. The Japanese central bank eventually lowered its interest rate almost to zero, but the economy remained extremely weak. It has only been in the years since 2004 that Japan's economy has again been showing respectable growth rates. This rebound was certainly aided by low interest rates, but it required many other policy changes as well.

This means that the Fed cannot always generate the rate of growth and level of employment that it considers best. But the Fed can prevent the economy from growing faster than it wants, and it can keep the economy from creating more jobs than it thinks are desirable.

Why would the Fed ever want to make the economy grow more slowly or have fewer jobs? The answer is that the Fed worries that if too many people have jobs, or if it is too easy for workers to find jobs, there will be upward pressure on wages. More rapid wage growth can get translated into more rapidly rising prices – in other words, inflation. So the Fed often decides to raise interest rates to slow the economy and keep people out of work in order to keep inflation from increasing and eventually getting out of control.

Most people probably do not realize that the Federal Reserve Board, an agency of the government, intervenes in the economy to prevent it from creating too many jobs. But there is even more to the story. When the Fed hits the brakes to slow job growth, it is not doctors, lawyers, and CEOs who end up without jobs. The people who lose are those in the middle and the bottom – sales clerks, factory workers, custodians, and dishwashers. These are the workers who don't get hired or get laid off when the economy slows or goes into a recession.

The unemployment rate for everyone rises when the economy goes into a downturn, but unemployment rises most for those with the least education. For example, at the peak of the last business cycle in 2000, the unemployment rate for workers with just a high school degree had fallen as low as 3.2 percent. It had risen by 2.5 percentage points to 5.7 percent by early 2003. By contrast, the unemployment rate for workers with college degrees rose by just 1.7 percentage points over the same period, topping out at 3.2 percent in 2003.[4]

African Americans and Hispanics also suffer disproportionately when the unemployment rate rises. The unemployment rate for white workers rose from 3.4 at its low in 2000 to 5.5 percent in 2003, an increase of 2.1 percentage points. By contrast, the unemployment rate rose by 3.3 percentage points for Hispanics, from a low of 5.1 percent in 2000 to 8.4 percent in 2003. For African Americans, the unemployment rate rose by 4.4 percentage points, from a low of 7 percent in 2000 to 11.4 percent in 2003. For African American teens unemployment nearly doubled from a low of 20 percent in 2000 to a high of 37.8 percent in 2003. This pattern is typical; as a rule of thumb, the unemployment rate for Hispanics is 1.5 times the overall unemployment rate, the unemployment rate for African Americans is twice the overall average, and the unemployment rate for African American teens is typically six times the overall average.

The rise in unemployment in the 2001 downturn was actually relatively small compared with prior recessions in which the impact on disadvantaged segments of the population was considerably more severe. The 1980-82 recessions caused the unemployment rate among whites to rise from a low of

---

[4] These numbers can found in the "Get Detailed Statistics" section of the Bureau of Labor Statistics website [http://www.bls.gov].

4.8 percent in 1979 to a high of 9.7 percent in 1982. The unemployment rate for Hispanics rose by 8.1 percentage points, from 7.6 percent in 1979 to 15.7 percent in 1982. The unemployment rate for African Americans increased from 11.7 percent in 1979 to a peak of 21.2 percent in 1983, a rise of 9.5 percentage points. The unemployment rate for African American teens jumped 17.7 percentage points, hitting a peak of 52 percent in 1983.

Of course, the Fed doesn't push up unemployment rates as an end in itself. It pushes up the unemployment rate to slow wage growth, and thereby relieve inflationary pressure. But the wages that grow more slowly are the wages of the workers who feel the biggest hit in terms of unemployment. When the overall unemployment rate fell below 5 percent and eventually to 4 percent in the late 1990s, wages for most workers were rising at a healthy pace. Real wages for workers with just a high school education increased by 5.5 percent between 1995 and 2000. By contrast, in the years of higher unemployment rates from 1989 to 1995, these workers saw their real wage fall by almost 2.0 percent.[5]

There was a similar story for African American and Hispanic workers. The real wage for a typical African American man rose by 8.9 percent in the five years from 1995 to 2000.[6] It had declined by 2.8 percent in the prior six years from 1989 to 1995. African American women saw a real wage gain of 11.2 percent in years of low unemployment, compared to a loss of 1.1 percent from 1989 to 1995. Hispanic men saw their real wages grow by 9.6 percent from 1995 to 2000, after falling by 8.9 percent in the prior six years. For Hispanic women, the difference was a wage gain of 6.4 percent in the years 1995 to 2000, compared with a loss of 2.0 percent from 1989 to 1995.

In periods of low unemployment, workers don't only gain from higher wages. Employers must make efforts to accommodate workers' various needs, such as child care or flexible work schedules, because they know that workers have other employment options. The Fed is well aware of the difficulties that employers face in periods of low unemployment. It compiles a regular survey, called the "Beige Book," of attitudes from around the country about the state of the economy. Most of the people interviewed for the Beige Book are employers.

From 1997 to 2000, when the unemployment rate was at its lowest levels in 30 years, the Beige Book was filled with complaints that some companies were pulling workers from other companies with offers of higher wages and better benefits. Some Beige Books reported that firms had to offer such non-wage benefits as flexible work hours, child care, or training in order to retain workers. The Beige Books give accounts of firms having to send buses into inner cities to bring workers out to the suburbs to work in hotels and restaurants. It even reported that some employers were forced to hire workers with handicaps in order to meet their needs for labor.

From the standpoint of employers, life is much easier when the workers are lined up at the door clamoring for jobs than when workers have the option to shop around for better opportunities. Employers can count on a sympathetic

---

[5] This is taken from Mishel et al. (2005, Table 2.17).
[6] The numbers in this paragraph are taken from Mishel et al. (Tables 2.24 and 2.25).

ear from the Fed. When the Fed perceives too much upward wage pressure, it slams on the brakes and brings the party to an end. The Fed justifies limiting job growth and raising the unemployment rate because of its concern that inflation may get out of control, but this does not change the fact that it is preventing workers, and specifically less-skilled workers, from getting jobs, and clamping down on their wage growth.

When Does the Fed Clamp Down?

As a general rule, it is probably safe to assume that lower unemployment rates are associated with more inflationary pressure than higher unemployment rates. Not only do workers have more bargaining power, but periods of low unemployment are also periods when the economy is strong generally and businesses will be more able to pass on higher costs (from wages or other sources) in higher prices. But there is no problem with modest rates of inflation. In fact, in 2002 the Fed was concerned (at least in public statements) about the possibility of deflation, or falling prices. The Fed clearly indicated that it was more comfortable with modest inflation (e.g. 1.0 percent to 2.0 percent) than the prospect of modest deflation. So the Fed doesn't clamp down just because there is a little bit of inflation, the Fed clamps down when it gets concerned that inflation is on the verge of getting out of control.

But even here there are no clear guidelines. Until the late 1990s, the conventional wisdom among economists was that if the unemployment rate fell below a certain level (most economists put the level in a range between 5.8 percent and 6.4 percent unemployment), the inflation rate would begin to increase. Furthermore, they believed that the inflation would continue to increase as long as the unemployment rate remained below this safe range.[7]

Alan Greenspan acted under this belief in 1994 when he raised the federal funds rate by a full 3 percentage points in just over a year, from 3 percent in February of 1994 to 6 percent by March of 1995. At the time he began raising interest rates, there was very little evidence in the data of any problems with inflation. Rather, Greenspan was engaging in what was termed a preemptive strike. The unemployment rate had been declining into the 5.8-6.4 percent range that was viewed as consistent with a steady pace of inflation. Greenspan and others were fearful that if the unemployment rate continued to decline to levels below this range, then inflation would begin to pick up. In order to prevent this from happening, Greenspan raised interest rates to slow the economy and job creation, thereby keeping the unemployment rate from reaching a level that he thought would lead to inflation. He had the backing of the vast majority of the economics profession in his actions at the time. In fact, the consensus on this view was so widespread at the time, that one prominent economist described

---

[7] This is "non-accelerating inflation rate of unemployment" or NAIRU theory. It holds that the inflation rate will increase if the unemployment rate is below the NAIRU (which had been estimated as being between 5.8 percent and 6.4 percent), and will decrease if the unemployment rate is above the NAIRU. For a more detailed discussion of this view see Bernstein and Baker (2004) and Galbraith (1998).

those who thought the unemployment rate could go lower without setting off inflation as "politically motivated hacks."[8]

However, later in the year, Greenspan broke with the consensus within the profession by lowering interest rates. In August of 1995 there was evidence that the economy was slowing. There also was no evidence that inflation was posing any problems, even though the unemployment rate was just 5.7 percent, a level at which most economists expected that low unemployment would lead to higher inflation. In this context, Greenspan decided to lower interest rates so that the economy could grow more quickly and the unemployment rate could fall further.

This is exactly what happened. Over the next 5 years, the unemployment rate continued to decline, averaging just 4 percent for all of 2000, the lowest level since 1969. Over this period, there was no notable uptick in the inflation rate, even though the unemployment rate fell to levels that economists had predicted would trigger escalating inflation. In other words, the bulk of the economics profession was proven to be badly mistaken by the events of the late nineties. If Greenspan had adhered to the orthodoxy in the economics profession, there would have been 5.4 million fewer people working in 2000 than was in fact the case and the nation's output for the year would have been approximately $400 billion lower than the level it actually reached in 2000.[9] The cumulative loss in output over the years from 1995 to 2000 would have been approximately $1 trillion, if Greenspan had followed the orthodoxy within the economics profession, and never allowed the unemployment rate to fall below 6.0 percent.

The importance of this brief digression into recent history is that economists really do not understand very well the process by which inflation gets to be a problem. Greenspan defied the economic orthodoxy when he allowed the unemployment rate to hit 30-year lows in the late nineties, and he turned out to be right. Almost any other mainstream economist in his position would have raised interest rates enough so that the unemployment rate would never have fallen much below 6.0 percent, depriving millions of workers of jobs and leading to a vast loss of economic production.[10] This episode is important to keep in mind when considering who controls the Fed – different people might pursue very different policies.

---

[8] See Krugman (1995).

[9] These calculations are derived using Okun's law that a 1.0 percentage point decline in the unemployment rate is associated with approximately a 2.0 percentage point increase in output. The implicit assumption is that there is roughly 1 percent counted as not being in the workforce who comes out of the woodworks to find a job for every person who goes from being unemployed to being employed.

[10] In fact, at the time Greenspan had to overcome the opposition of Janet Yellen and Lawrence Meyers, the two most prominent economists on the Fed's Board of Governors, in getting the Fed to keep interest rates low and allow unemployment to fall.

The Fed: Who Calls the Shots?

While it can be hard to follow the mechanism through which the Fed affects the economy, it can be even harder to figure out who actually controls the policy at the Federal Reserve Board. The Federal Reserve Board chairman — currently Ben Bernanke, but Alan Greenspan for most of the last 18 years — has enormous power over the Fed's policy decisions, but this is only part of the story.

For the last quarter century, the Federal Reserve Board has been dominated by chairmen who came to be highly regarded in political circles and who were almost always able to get their way in determining the direction of Fed policy. However, under the law, the key policy decisions on interest rates by the Federal Reserve Board are made by the Fed's Open Market Committee. This committee has 18 members, 12 of whom are voting members. Seven of the voting members, including the Federal Reserve Board chair, are members of the Fed's Board of Governors. These seven governors are appointed by the president for 14-year terms and are approved by the Senate. (The term as chair is 4 years.)

The other five voting members of the Open Market Committee are selected from the 12 presidents of the Fed's district banks. (The president of the New York district bank is always a voting member of the Open Market Committee.) All 12 district bank presidents sit on the Open Market Committee and take part in discussions. The district bank presidents in turn are selected through a process that is largely controlled by the banks in the district.[11] This means that five of the 12 people who have a vote on the nation's monetary policy are not appointed by democratically elected officials.

The composition of the Open Market Committee matters to the public because different people can reach very different conclusions about when it is desirable for the Fed to take actions to slow the economy. Some differences in policy can stem from differences in how people understand the economy. As noted earlier, Greenspan had a different view of the economy from most mainstream economists in the mid- and late-nineties when he allowed the unemployment rate to fall to levels that most economists thought would trigger serious problems with inflation. At this point, there are a wide range of views among economists about when inflation is likely to pose a problem and how seriously the Fed should respond to modest increases in the inflation rate.

There are also real grounds for informed people to have different views of the tradeoffs between the risk of inflation and higher unemployment. Bankers are likely to be less concerned about a 1 to 2 percentage point rise in the unemployment rate than autoworkers, sales clerks, or custodians. It is unlikely that many bankers, or their friends and family members, will lose their jobs if the unemployment rate were to increase by this amount. Nor are their wages

---

[11] A full description of the district banks and the rules for appointing their governments can be found in Section 4 of the Federal Reserve Act, which is available on the Fed's website [http://www.federalreserve.gov/generalinfo/fract/].

likely to suffer substantially from higher unemployment. As noted earlier, the people who feel both the higher unemployment and experience slower wage growth are disproportionately workers in the middle and bottom of the income distribution.

On the other hand, bankers may be very concerned about modest increases in the rate of inflation. They lend money at fixed interest rates. If the inflation rate rises above the rate they anticipated when they made loans, then the bankers will be repaid in money that is worth less than the money they lent. In other words, higher than expected inflation rates cut directly into bank profits. Businesses can also be unhappy if workers are in a position to push up their wages or demand better benefits because the unemployment rate is low. Workers can easily find another job when unemployment is low, so it puts pressure on employers to accommodate the needs of workers. Of course, businesses also benefit from having strong growth in demand since this increases their sales and typically their profits, so they are likely to be more mixed in their views of the trade-off between the risk of higher inflation and higher unemployment.

For these reasons, it is likely to matter a great deal that the financial sector has a grossly disproportionate influence in determining Fed policy. Representatives of the financial sector are likely to be quicker to raise interest rates and throw people out of work than people who represent the working population or even the business sector as a whole.

It is also possible that people who answer to the larger working population, rather than just financial interests and to some extent the business community, might try to look at alternatives to higher unemployment as a way to keep inflation under control. Prior to the eighties, political figures of both major parties applied a variety of wage-price guidelines and/or controls to slow inflation.[12] Economists have come to view these measures as both inefficient and largely ineffective in stemming inflation. While this assessment of wage-price guidelines and controls may well prove accurate, the policy pushed by mainstream economists in the nineties (of not letting the unemployment rate fall below 6 percent) would have led to huge economic and social costs if Greenspan had followed it. In other words, the mechanism that economists propose for controlling inflation is enormously costly to the economy as a whole, and especially to the bottom 60-70 percent of the income distribution. Therefore it is reasonable to search for other mechanisms, even if these mechanisms may also carry some economic costs.

In this respect, it is worth noting that there is now an extensive economic literature examining the trade-off between unemployment and labor market institutions like unions, employment protection laws, and unemployment benefits.[13] One of the strongest results in this literature is that coordinated bargaining agreements between large groups of workers and employers and/or

---

[12] Richard Nixon actually put in place wage-price controls over most sectors of the economy when he was president.

[13] See Baker et al. (2004).

the government is associated with lower rates of unemployment. This system, which exists most strongly in some northern European countries like Sweden, the Netherlands, and Ireland, allows workers to directly gauge the impact of their wage demands on the economy and adjust them accordingly. It has allowed several of these countries to sustain unemployment rates that are lower than those in the United States, without any notable problems with inflation.

Of course, these countries have very different histories than the United States, and perhaps most importantly they are countries in which the overwhelming majority of the workforce is represented by union contracts. By contrast, less than 10 percent of the private sector work force is represented by union contracts in the United States. This means that switching over to this system of coordinated bargaining in the United States would not be an easy task, since the United States doesn't have the institutional structure to support it.

But even if it turns out that there is no alternative to using high unemployment to keep inflation under control, it is important to remember that different people will assess the risk of higher inflation and the cost of higher unemployment very differently. The fact that the people with the most say in determining Fed policy are associated with the financial sector lends a strong anti-inflation bias to Fed policy. The financial sector is willing to force workers to endure the costs of higher unemployment in order to minimize the risks of inflation. If the Fed were run by people who more closely represented the interests of the public as a whole, it would likely be willing to tolerate greater risks of inflation in order to lower the unemployment rate.

Finally, we should clearly recognize the hand of government in the Fed's policy decisions. Because our economists are not smart enough to find a better way to contain inflation, they deliberately keep millions of people from holding jobs in order to maintain downward pressure on the wages of less-skilled workers. This Fed generated unemployment is a big source of downward pressure on the wages of tens of millions of workers in the modern economy. The wages of CEOs, doctors, and lawyers do not suffer much when the Fed pushes up interest rates; the wages and employment prospects of autoworkers, store clerks, and dishwashers do suffer when the Fed raises rates.

Alan Greenspan, like his predecessor Paul Volcker, enjoyed a reputation as an inflation fighter. Both were quick to raise interest rates at various points in their tenure to choke off inflation. We can debate whether their interest rate hikes were always necessary to stem inflation, but what is not subject to debate is who constituted the army for these generals in the war against inflation. The core units of the army were composed of the millions of workers who ended up without jobs because Volcker or Greenspan deliberately slowed the pace of job creation. The larger army included the tens of millions of workers who ended up with lower pay and benefits or worse job conditions because their employment opportunities were limited by Volcker and Greenspan's actions. It's fine if people want to praise Volcker and Greenspan for their wise conduct of monetary policy, but we should at least have the decency to recognize the tens of millions of workers who made sacrifices so that their policies would be effective.

We should also recognize that the millions without jobs and the tens of millions with falling wages are not suffering because of the market. They are suffering because Paul Volcker, Alan Greenspan, or Benjamin Bernanke could not think of a better way to control inflation.

CHAPTER THREE

The Secret of High CEO Pay and Other Mysteries of the Corporation

According to the conservative nanny state mythology (both the creationist and intelligent design variants), corporations were set on the earth at the same time as humans. They peacefully co-existed in the state of nature until the government stepped in and tried to interfere with the natural order by doing things like regulating and taxing corporations. The nanny state conservatives want the government to step back and allow corporations a freer hand to do what comes naturally: make profits. They rant about the threat posed by government regulation, and even worse "double taxation" – the fact that corporate profits are taxed when corporations earn the money, and then also taxed when they are paid out as dividends to shareholders.

The mythology may be moving, emotionally and politically, but it suffers both as a historical account and in its logic. To get a realistic view of the relationship between the government, corporations, and society, it's necessary to discard the conservative nanny state mythology about the origins of corporations and apply a little common sense. However painful it may be to the nanny state conservatives, a serious discussion must begin with a basic truth: the corporation does not exist in a free market, it is a creation of the government.

Why Governments Create Corporations

The fact that corporations are a creation of the government is not debatable. In the absence of government intervention, individuals are free to do any sort of business deals they want. They trade goods, buy and sell labor, lend money, form partnerships, and engage in an almost infinite variety of transactions. But they cannot form a corporation – a legal entity that exists independently of its owners. This requires the government.

Corporations are a great invention of government. They make it possible to raise vast amounts of capital for major business ventures like building car factories, laying telecommunications lines, or operating an airline. Corporations can raise capital far more effectively than business partnerships because the government gives them the privilege of limited liability. This means that the owners of the corporation, its shareholders, only stand to lose what they have invested in a company's stock. They cannot be held personally liable for any debts of the company if the company ends up in bankruptcy.

This means, for example, that if a company that engages in accounting fraud, like Enron or WorldCom, ends up owing its suppliers and creditors billions of dollars more than its assets can cover, the individual shareholders do not risk losing their homes or bank accounts. Their only loss is what they invested in Enron stock. The same principle applies to companies that may have destroyed their workers' health by exposing them to asbestos, while concealing evidence that the material was extremely dangerous. Stockholders also don't have to worry about their personal assets if General Motors, Ford, or United Airlines can't make good on their commitments to their workers' pensions and retirement health care benefits. They can only lose the money that they have invested in the company's stock, and not a penny more.

If these companies had merely been groups of individuals, not corporations with stockholders, then all of the owners would be personally liable for making good on contractual commitments that they had made and the damage they had caused. They could be forced to surrender their home, their personal assets, and their savings in order to pay off debts resulting from their business operations. It takes a conservative nanny state to create an institution, like a corporation, that allows investors to cause harm and not be held accountable.

Historically, the government issued charters of incorporation only to advance specific public purposes. In England, a company could only gain a charter of incorporation through a special act of Parliament. These charters were usually issued to companies involved in the building and maintenance of transportation routes. In the 18th century this typically meant canals and turnpikes. In the first half of the 19th century, railroads were the main recipients of charters of incorporation. Parliament also gave charters of incorporation to the big trading companies that England established to promote trade in its colonies: the British East India Company and the South Sea Company. England did not have laws setting out general rules of incorporation until 1844. Prior to that point, a company seeking corporate status had to apply for a special act of Parliament.

The United States adopted laws creating general rules for incorporation somewhat earlier, with New York leading the way in 1811.[1] The states had originally accepted the English approach to corporate status, restricting it to companies that were felt to be performing a specific public purpose. However, a burst of industrialization around the War of 1812 created an environment in which many companies wanted the benefits of corporate status in order to make it easier to raise capital.

The logic of creating general rules of incorporation actually directly followed the prior logic of granting corporate status only for specific purposes. The basis for setting general rules under which anyone can establish a corporation is that there is a general public interest in promoting wealth, and corporations exist to increase wealth. Therefore, the government is granting a special privilege in order to advance a public good.

---

[1] The adoption of general laws of incorporation is discussed in Blackford (1998) and Horwitz (1997).

The Gift Giver Gets to Set the Rules

The gift of limited liability is a hugely valuable benefit from the government to corporations and their shareholders.[2] The immediate evidence for the value of corporate status is the money raised from the corporate income tax ($278 billion in 2005).[3] The corporate income tax is an entirely voluntary tax. The government does not force anyone to establish a corporation. Any group of individuals engaged in a business operation are free to organize themselves as a partnership, which would not require them to pay the corporate income tax, they would only be liable for individual income taxes. The fact that businesses have voluntarily chosen to organize themselves as corporations means that they view the benefits of corporate status to be greater than the burden of the corporate income tax. All of the country's major corporations (or their shareholders) have effectively voted with their feet. They all believe that the benefits that the conservative nanny state gives them by allowing them to establish corporations must be at least as large as the taxes that the government imposes on corporations.

The fact that the government is giving something of great value when it allows firms to incorporate is very important when considering the rules that the government imposes on corporations. In effect, the rules placed on corporate conduct are part of quid pro quo involved in establishing a corporation. The reason that the government allows individuals to form corporations is that it wants to facilitate economic growth, but the government will be less effective in promoting this goal if it does not put in place the right set of rules for corporate governance.

As it stands, there are already extensive sets of rules regarding corporate governance. The government imposes a long list of requirements on corporations regarding issues such as financial disclosure, elections of corporate boards, and protection of minority shareholders. Most of these rules are not controversial; they are seen as laying the groundwork for the effective operation of a modern market economy. There would be few people anxious to buy shares in a company if they couldn't obtain financial information on the company and have some assurance that its reported profits, assets, and liabilities were accurate measures of its financial situation. In the same vein, if the majority of shareholders (or whoever happened to take control of the company) were able to seize the wealth of the company, and leave nothing for the rest of the shareholders, few people would want to risk buying stock. Government

---

[2] Limited liability is not the only benefit of corporate status. The corporate structure allows shareholders to freely come and go in a way that would not be possible with a partnership (the other partners may place restrictions on when and how a partner could dispose of her interest in the partnership). The corporate structure also allows individuals to preserve anonymity in a way that is not often possible in a partnership. This can allow individuals to invest in ways that they may not want publicly known, for example, owning shares in companies that distribute pornography or sell tobacco. Corporate share ownership allows anonymity in ways that are not in general possible in a partnership.

[3] Congressional Budget Office (2006, Table 4-2).

rules on corporate governance prevent such events, and thereby give the public assurance about the soundness of investing in shares of stock.

This is useful background in thinking about high CEO pay. What is it that allowed Michael Eisner to earn $680 million in the years from 1998 to 2000 when he was the CEO of the Disney Corporation, or Robert Grasso to pocket $140 million from running the New York Stock Exchange? The conservative nanny state crew wants us to believe that it was their incredible skill and hard work that allowed these CEOs to earn such vast sums. The more obvious answer is that badly designed rules of corporate governance allow CEOs to pilfer large amounts of money from the corporations they manage, because there is no one with both the interest and power to challenge them.

CEO pay has exploded in the last quarter century, rising far more rapidly than either the pay of typical workers or the overall rate of productivity growth. The average pay of a corporate CEO was less than 40 times the pay of a typical worker in the late seventies. This ratio rose to 300 to 1 at the peak of the stock bubble in the late nineties, as the value of compensation packages heavily laden with stock options went through the roof. But even as the stock market has fallen back to more reasonable levels, CEO pay is still close to 200 times the pay of a typical worker.[4]

This explosion in CEO pay is not tied in any obvious way to their effective management, even by the narrow measure of increasing corporate profits. A recent study that examined the pay of the top five executives in 1500 corporations found that the pay over the period 1993-2003 increased almost twice as rapidly as could be explained by profit growth or other standard measures of corporate success (Bebchuk and Grinstein, 2005).

Furthermore, this explosion in CEO pay is almost exclusively an American phenomenon. There has been no comparable increase in CEO pay in Canadian, European, or Japanese corporations. The pay of CEOs in the United States in 2003 was 2.5 times the average pay of CEOs in Canada, more than 3 times the pay of CEOs in France, and almost five times the average pay of CEOS in Japan.[5] It would be difficult to argue that foreign corporations have been poorly managed by incompetent CEOs in an era in which they have managed to seize market share from their U.S. competitors in the auto industry, the aerospace industry, and other large sectors of the economy.

CEO pay in the United States has exploded for the simple reason that CEOs largely get to write their own checks. CEO pay is determined by corporate compensation boards, most of the members of which are put there with the blessing of the CEOs themselves. Usually the CEOs have a large voice in determining who sits on the corporate boards that ultimately have responsibility for the operation of the corporation. These corporate boards then appoint a committee that determines CEO pay. In effect, we allow the CEO to pick a group of friends to decide how much money he should earn. When they

---

[4] These data are taken from Mishel et al. (2005, Figure 2-25).

[5] Mishel et al. (2005, Table 2.47).

42

are sitting on the boards of corporations that control tens of billions of dollars in revenue, their friends are likely to be very generous.

In principle, the shareholders can organize and put in place directors who will take a harder line on CEO pay, but organizing shareholders is a very time-consuming process, it's just like running a campaign for public office. Furthermore, most corporate charters stack the deck against anyone seeking to challenge management's plans. They allow the company to count stock proxies that are not returned as votes in support of management's position.

This hugely tilts the scales in any election in favor of management. It is comparable to allowing political incumbents to count all the people who don't turn out to vote as voting in their favor. Few challengers would win elections under these rules. Similarly, there are not many occasions where outsiders can overturn corporate management's decisions, especially on something like CEO pay, which will not make that much difference on the bottom line.[6] It's much easier to just sell the stock if you don't like what's going on.

Interestingly, the nanny state conservatives do believe that there are situations in which seemingly democratic institutions can produce unfair outcomes. The nanny state conservatives have launched efforts nationally, and in several states, to change the terms under which union officials can use members' funds in political campaigns. Under the law, it is illegal to use union dues for political campaigns, however, unions can use voluntary contributions from their members for this purpose. Unions often assess their members' fees for the union's political action committee. Under many contracts, these fees can be directly deducted from workers' paychecks, but they are refundable to members who request that their money not be used for political campaigns.

Many nanny state conservatives have argued that this arrangement is not fair to union members, since many may object to having their money used for political campaigns, but may not be willing to take the time and effort to get a refund. The nanny state conservatives argue that the union should only be able to get money from members who have explicitly indicated that they want the union to get their money. This switch, from the default being that the union gets the money to the default being that the union doesn't get the money, would probably have a substantial impact on the amount of money collected.

The extent to which this switch would affect the ability of unions to be important actors in political campaigns is not important in this context, what is important is that the nanny state conservatives are very much aware of how changes in the ground rules can affect the balance of power. In a world where corporate CEOs can virtually write their own paychecks, there is something seriously wrong with the balance of power.

---

[6] Even the highest CEO salaries tend not to be very large relative to corporate revenue or even corporate profit. For example, in the years from 1998-2000, when Michael Eisner pocketed $680 million as CEO of Disney, after-tax profits of the Disney corporation were almost $11 billion. This means that if Eisner's pay had been reduced by 90 percent, it would have only boosted profits by 6 percent. This increase is not trivial, but Eisner's compensation package was extreme, even in a world of hugely inflated CEO pay.

To redress this imbalance, we can just steal an item from the nanny state conservative's agenda. They called their measure to require unions to get explicit permission from workers to deduct money from their paycheck for political campaigns the "paycheck protection act." In the same vein, to keep a rein on CEO pay, it would be a simple matter to require that the pay packages for the top 5-10 executives be submitted to shareholders at regular intervals for approval. In this vote, share proxies that are not returned would not count, so that the pay package would actually have to win majority approval among those voting.[7] Perhaps Michael Eisner would still be able to earn hundred million dollar paychecks with these new rules, but the deck would be less heavily stacked in his favor.

There is a better argument to require this sort of shareholder majority voting rule than for the paycheck protection act. After all, union officers are directly or indirectly elected by a democratic vote of their members, in which non-voters do not count. Also, it is much easier to sell stock than change jobs. Since workers will be reluctant to change jobs, union members who are unhappy with the way their union is run have far more incentive to get involved than do shareholders who are unhappy with the way their corporation is run. There would seem to be a much more pressing need to rebalance the scales in corporate elections than in union paycheck deductions – that is, if the nanny state conservatives were actually concerned about matters of principle.

But the more important issue is that the government can and must set the rules for corporate governance. The government creates corporations and sets the rules under which they operate. This is essential, and, as noted earlier, is for the benefit of the corporations themselves. No one would buy shares in a corporation if he or she thought that the management was free to simply steal their money.

For a variety of reasons, the mechanisms that once placed a check on the ability of corporate management to pilfer money for its own use have broken down. This may be partly attributable to the spread of share ownership, so that instances where a single family maintains control of a major corporation (and therefore can keep its management in line) are less common. It may also be partly attributable to changing morals in the larger society, so that unchecked greed is more acceptable. But the causes of the breakdown don't matter as much as the remedies. And the most effective remedies are changing the rules to ensure that CEO power is held in check.

It is possible that the requirement that all CEO pay packages must be stated explicitly and approved by a majority of shareholders would not be

---

[7] Actually, it would be a reasonable policy to require that all proxy votes be decided by a majority of those voting. Management always enjoys a substantial advantage in access to information, the ability to disseminate information to shareholders, and setting the timing of proxy votes. There is no obvious justification for also giving them the benefit of the votes of those who do not take the time to return their proxies. Ensuring that key corporate decisions and officers better represent the shareholders could lead to better corporate management. It might also be reasonable to require that long-term employees gain representation on corporate boards, but that is an issue best left for another book.

sufficient to rein in CEO pay. There are additional measures to help rein in CEO pay; for example, corporations could tie incentive pay, such as stock options, to the performance of the industry group as a whole. There is no reason that the CEO of Exxon-Mobil deserves a huge pay increase because the price of oil has tripled, sending the price of Exxon-Mobil stock through the roof along with the stock price of all other oil companies. For some reason, the idea that CEO performance can be best judged in comparison with a reference group has apparently not occurred to most executive compensation committees.

In the same vein, it might be reasonable to cap total stock-linked compensation, or impose a schedule that is likely to limit truly exorbitant payouts. It is possible that some CEOs will walk away if they know that their compensation from their work is limited to $50 million a year, but there are probably not too many CEOs in this situation. Similarly, if compensation packages were structured so that CEOs only got half of the gain on their stock options once they passed $20 million, or one-fifth of the gain once they passed $50 million, most CEOs would probably still take the job.

The key to containing CEO compensation is not laws from Congress that mandate lower pay; the best route is changing the rules that determine the accountability that corporate directors have to shareholders. Congress has changed these rules often in the past. For example, in 1995 it passed legislation that made it more difficult for shareholders to sue corporate directors or officers for stock manipulation, in effect substantially increasing the power of corporate management relative to its shareholders.[8] If the law explicitly stated that corporate boards have an obligation to contain CEO pay to market levels, and that directors could be held personally liable for failing to take this responsibility seriously, then the growth of CEO pay would likely be much lower in the future. This would not involve the government stepping in and determining CEO salaries. Rather, shareholders would use the courts to obtain compensation from corporate directors who did not take their responsibilities seriously, and who wrote a blank check to the CEO.

Of course, it is also important to keep in mind that any changes in corporate governance would be voluntary for shareholders. If the new rules prove unacceptable to them for whatever reason, they would have the same option that they have now to reconstitute their business as a partnership and apply whatever governance rules they consider best. But if they want the privileges that the government grants to corporations, then they have to be prepared to abide by the rules that the government sets.

---

[8] In 1995, Congress passed the "Private Securities Litigation Reform Act," which made it far more difficult to prove a case of stock price manipulation; essentially, the law required actual evidence in the form of a conversation or written document showing that an officer or director had actively manipulated the stock price. Patterns in the movement of stock prices and stock transactions by specific officers or directors would not be a sufficient basis for a suit. The bill was vetoed by President Clinton, but Congress overrode his veto.

Moving Beyond Double Taxation

Once we recognize that granting corporate status is a benefit granted by the government to shareholders, then the whining of the nanny state conservatives about double-taxation takes on a very different appearance. There is no "double-taxation" taking place. The corporate income tax is essentially a fee that shareholders pay the government in exchange for the benefits of corporate status. If they don't feel that the benefits of corporate status are as large as the income tax that the corporation must pay, then they are free to reconstitute their corporation as a partnership. Every corporation that does not become a partnership has opted to pay the corporate income tax rather than surrender the privileges of corporate status.

It is understandable that shareholders do not want their corporations to pay tax, and they don't want to pay taxes on their dividend and capital gain income. Most people would rather not pay tax at all. People would also rather not pay for their food, electricity, or home mortgage. But in the real world, there are no free lunches. If the government collects less money from corporate taxes, then it must collect more money through other taxes. The corporate income tax is a relatively progressive tax, since taxes on corporate profits come primarily out of the pockets of shareholders, and stock is held disproportionately by the wealthy. It also has the advantage of being voluntary, since no one is forced to hold shares in a corporation. Given that the government needs revenue, a voluntary progressive tax like the corporate income tax is probably a good place to start.

CHAPTER FOUR

Bill Gates – Welfare Mom

How Government Patent and Copyright Monopolies Enrich the Rich and Distort the Economy

Bill Gates, with his rise from modest affluence to incredible wealth, is one of the heroes of the conservative nanny state. A clever college dropout, he foresaw the massive growth of information technology and developed the computer operating systems that control the vast majority of personal computers in use around the world. As a result of his extraordinary insight and impressive business sense, he became the richest person in the world, amassing a fortune that approached $80 billion at one point. Now he is devoting much of his fortune and his energy to aiding the world's poor, financing research into the treatment of tropical diseases, and paying for millions of poor people to get vaccines and treatment that they could not otherwise afford.

This is powerful mythology, but the story leaves out the key role of the conservative nanny state in making Bill Gates the richest man in the world. Mr. Gates was only able to amass his incredible fortune because of copyright protection on software: a government-granted monopoly. Of course, copyright protection, like its cousin, patent protection, serves a purpose. It provides incentives to innovate and do creative work; this part of the story will be discussed in a moment. But first it is necessary to fully appreciate what copyright and patent protection mean.

Do Free Markets Have Government Imposed Monopolies?

In a free market, individuals can make any exchanges they choose. They can sell the things they grow, the things their make, their labor, their ideas, or anything else that finds a willing buyer. Copyrights and patents give their holders government-enforced monopolies that restrict free exchange. The government will not allow someone to sell their copy of Windows (at least not without Bill Gate's permission) because it has given Microsoft a monopoly on the sale of this product, through copyright protection. Similarly, the government will arrest anyone who produces a drug on which Merck or Eli Lilly holds a patent. It is only because of the government's enforcement of these monopolies that Microsoft is a hugely profitable company and Bill Gates is an incredibly rich person. The same situation applies to patent protection in the pharmaceutical industry, and copyright protection in the entertainment industry. Vast segments of the economy are dependent on government-enforced monopolies for their profitability and survival.

Whether or not copyright protection is a desirable public policy, it is undeniably a huge government intervention in the market. In the case of prescription drugs, patent monopolies raise the average price of protected drugs

47

by more than 200 percent, and in some cases by as much as 5,000 percent.[1] In the case of copyright protection, items like software and recorded music and movies that would otherwise be available at zero cost over the Internet, can instead be sold for hundreds of dollars. Clearly these forms of protection are substantial interventions in the economy.

The fact that copyright and patent protections are forms of intervention does not mean that they are bad, but it is essential to at least recognize this fact in order to assess their merits. Suppose we eliminated all welfare to needy mothers in the form of cash benefits from the government, and instead assigned them the right to control traffic intersections in major cities. Then we allowed these poor mothers to charge people to make turns from the intersections. These women could have the police arrest anyone who crosses the intersection under their control without paying them their royalty, just as Bill Gates will have the police arrest anyone who sells Windows without paying him a royalty. The royalties they collect could provide enough income to support them without any money from the government. In this way, we could get rid of welfare – the classic big government social program – and still ensure that poor mothers have the income needed to support their family.

Giving people the right to charge royalties to cross intersections is government intervention in the economy and is every bit as much "big government" as if the government taxed people and redistributed the money to low-income mothers. It would not change anything if we declared the right to charge fees at an intersection a "copyright." Government intervention by any other name is government intervention.

The difference between Bill Gates' copyrights and the "copyrights" that control traffic intersections is that the government allowed Bill Gates to gain copyright protection ostensibly to reward him for his innovative work in developing software. (The other big difference is that Bill Gates, or, to be more accurate, Microsoft, collects much more money from copyright protection than needy mothers get from Temporary Assistance to Needy Families (TANF), the main government welfare program. In 2005, Microsoft's revenue was almost $40 billion, the vast majority of which it received as a result of its copyright protection for Windows and other software programs. By contrast, the federal government spent less than $18 billion on TANF in 2005.)[2] One of the policies of the conservative nanny state is to give copyright and patent monopolies as a reward for creative or innovative work. This may or may not be a good policy for the economy or society, but copyrights and patents are clearly forms of

---

[1] According to the Chain Drug Store Association, the average price of a brand drug in 2004 was $95.86 compared to $28.71 for a generic. These figures can be found in U.S. Census Bureau. 2006. *Statistical Abstract of the United States,* Washington, DC: Table 126).

[2] Data on Microsoft's 2005 revenue can be found in its quarterly report, available at [http://www.microsoft.com/msft/earnings/FY06/earn_rel_q1_06.mspx]. Data on the recent pattern of federal spending on TANF can be found in Coven. M. 2005. "An Introduction to TANF," Washington, DC: Center on Budget and Policy Priorities, [http://www.cbpp.org/1-22-02tanf2.htm].

government intervention in the economy that have substantial distributional effects.

The government is not obligated to award patent and copyright protection; it only makes sense if these are the best ways to promote innovation and creativity. In fact, this is exactly how the U.S. constitution discusses patents and copyrights. They are not listed as rights in the Bill of Rights, like freedom of speech or the free exercise of religion; patents and copyrights are implicitly referred to in Article 1, Section 8, where the Constitution lists the powers of Congress. The Constitution says, "To promote the progress of science and useful arts, by securing for limited times to authors and inventors the exclusive right to their respective writings and discoveries." The Constitution does not say that Congress must issue copyrights or patents, it simply has the power to do so, as a means "to promote the progress of science and useful arts." If Congress determines that there are more effective ways to promote innovation and creativity then it is not obligated to allow copyrights or patents, just as it is not obligated to levy taxes, if it determines that the country does not need the revenue.

Copyright and patent protections don't just make Bill Gates and Microsoft rich. They also make Michael Jackson, Britney Spears, and Arnold Schwarzenegger rich. Copyright and patent protection support a $220 billion a year prescription drug industry, a $25 billion medical supply industry, a $12 billion recorded music industry, a $25 billion movie industry, and a $12 billion textbook industry. According to the International Intellectual Property Alliance, industries that rely heavily on copyright and patent protection accounted for $630 billion of value added in 2002, almost 6 percent of the size of the economy. Without this nanny state intervention, the protected products (e.g. software, recorded music and videos, textbooks, prescription drugs, and high tech medical supplies) would be sold at a small fraction of their current price, or in many cases would be available at no cost over the Internet.

The promoters of the conservative nanny state claim that we would not have any innovation or creative work without these forms of government intervention. This is not true. There are other ways to support innovation and creative work; the question is, which mechanisms are the most efficient ones?

Efficient Mechanisms for Supporting Innovation and Creative Work

While it is not easy to determine the most efficient mechanisms for supporting innovation and creative work, it is not difficult to identify the key issues involved. The first part of the story is measuring the costs associated with maintaining patent and copyright protection instead of allowing free competition. The way to measure the static economic losses that result from the higher prices charged on patent and copyright-protected items is exactly the same method that economists use to measure the losses that result from trade protection like tariffs and quotas. The main difference is that the size of the losses are much larger in the case of patent and copyright protection. While tariffs or quotas on imports rarely raise the prices of the protected items by more than 15-20 percent, patents and copyrights raise the prices of protected products by several hundred percent, or more.

For example, patent-protected brand drugs sell for more than three times the price of generic drugs that sell in a free market.[3] This means that the country could save approximately $140 billion a year on its $220 billion annual bill for prescription drugs if the government did not provide patent protection and drugs were instead sold in a competitive market. In addition to raising the price for people who buy drugs, the higher patent protected price makes many people unable to afford drugs. These people either go without certain drugs or use less than their prescribed dosage because of government patent protection.

The fact that so many people can afford to buy drugs at the free market price, but cannot afford them at the patent protected price, is one of the inefficiencies of the patent system. This cost is known by economists as "deadweight loss." Economists usually get upset over deadweight losses when they are the result of a 10 percent tariff on pants or a quota on shirts. However, they are generally less troubled by the deadweight losses associated with patent and copyright protection, even when the losses are far more than the losses due to trade protection.

By raising prices above the competitive market price, patent protection also leads to a black market in unauthorized versions of prescription drugs. To a large extent this black market takes the form of drugs that are imported from countries that have lower prices. This can raise issues of drug quality for patients. While drugs imported from other rich countries with high safety standards, like Canada or Germany, are unlikely to pose problems, drugs imported from developing countries may be of more questionable quality. However, this flow of unauthorized imports is inevitable when a government enforced monopoly causes drugs to sell at prices far above their free market price. The government will be no more effective in eliminating this flow of imports than it has been in eliminating illegal drugs like marijuana or cocaine, or the Soviet Union was in preventing black market sales of blue jeans.

The pharmaceutical industry justifies the vast economic waste associated with patent protection for prescription drugs by claiming that patents are necessary to finance research. According to the pharmaceutical industry, it spent $41.1 billion on research in the United States in 2004.[4] This means that the country spends more than three dollars in higher drug prices for every dollar of drug research supported through the patent system. The rest of the additional spending went to marketing, high CEO pay, and drug company profits.

But this picture is still far too generous to the patent system. As any good economist would be quick to point out, government patent monopolies provide perverse incentives to pharmaceutical companies. They want to maximize the profits from these monopolies, which leads them to waste resources in ways that would not make sense in a free market.

---

[3] See footnote 1.
[4] This is taken from Pharmaceutical Research and Manufacturers of America (2005, figure 1.1).

One way that the pharmaceutical industry wastes resources is by engaging in copycat research, spending tens of billions of dollars developing drugs that duplicate the functions of already existing drugs. For example, once Pfizer developed Claritin, other drug companies rushed to develop comparable drugs to cash in on Pfizer's multi-billion dollar market. This behavior makes sense when a government-granted patent monopoly allows Pfizer to sell Claritin at a price that is much higher than its cost of production. (Copycat drugs actually are desirable in a world with patent protection, since they provide some competition in an environment where there would otherwise be none.) However, if Claritin were sold in a competitive market, it would make little sense to spend money developing a new drug that did the same thing as Claritin.

According to the Food and Drug Administration, approximately two-thirds of all new drugs fall into this copycat category.[5] The pharmaceutical industry estimates that copycat drugs cost approximately 90 percent as much to research as breakthrough drugs, which means that approximately 60 percent of the industry's spending on research is to develop copycat drugs (Ernst & Young LLP, 2001). This means instead of getting $40 billion in research on breakthrough drugs for the $140 billion that patents add to drug costs, we are only getting about $17 billion. In other words, we spend more than $8 in higher drug prices for every dollar that the industry spends researching breakthrough drugs.[6]

The monopoly profits that firms earn from patent protection also provide an incentive to misrepresent or conceal research findings. The corruption of the research process has created a major problem for medical journals, since researchers often have a financial stake in their results. In fact, in many cases, researchers have submitted articles to journals that they did not write. Rather, they were paid to lend their name to an article written by a pharmaceutical company. Newspapers are filled with accounts of drug companies that have concealed or distorted research findings that reflected negatively on their products.[7] When a company has billions of dollars at stake in marketing a particular drug, it has an enormous incentive to keep it on the market, even if there is evidence that the drug is less effective than the company claims, or may even be harmful.

---

[5] This reflects the percent of new drug approvals that are rated as "standard" as opposed to "priority," see U.S. Food and Drug Administration (2001).

[6] Copycat drugs do provide some benefits. Some patients have bad reactions to one drug, but may be able to take a copycat drug without any complications. Also, some drugs interact poorly, so it is often desirable to have a choice of drugs to treat a particular condition. However, as a general rule, the third, fourth, or fifth drug designed to treat a specific condition will provide far less medical benefit than a breakthrough drug that provides a treatment or cure where one did not previously exist.

[7] Merck, the manufacturer of the arthritis pain medication, Vioxx, has already lost two multi-million dollar lawsuits over the claim that it concealed evidence that the drug led to heart problems. Another recent example of patent rents discouraging manufacturers from revealing potential health problems was a heart implant device produced by Guidant, see "Guidant Debated Device Peril," New York Times, January 20, 2006.

The economic distortions created by patent monopolies permeate the research process itself, leading to rapidly growing costs. Joe DiMasi, the leading analyst of drug industry research costs, has documented this extraordinary run-up over the last two decades. DiMasi found that drug industry research costs have been rising by 11 percent a year (approximately 8 percent annually after adjusting for inflation) since 1987 (2003). While exploding costs may not be surprising in an industry with patent monopolies, it is striking in a sector that saw a vast increase in the supply of researchers worldwide due to the growth of countries like India and Brazil, as well as plunging prices for research tools like computers.

In a free market, companies have incentives to locate their research wherever its costs are lowest. However, in a world where governments grant patent monopolies, companies can use their location decisions as a way to pressure governments to allow them to charge higher prices. According to Sidney Taurel, the president and CEO of Eli Lilly, the pharmaceutical industry moved most of its research out of France to the United States because France places price controls on prescription drugs, and the United States grants firms unrestricted patent monopolies.[8] Since the location of research doesn't affect what pharmaceutical companies can charge in either France or the United States, the industry presumably relocated its research to punish France and/or reward the United States.

In the same vein, the industry has made statements that it will not locate research in developing countries unless they adopt strong patent protections. In other words, the industry is not locating its research where it will minimize research costs, it is using location decisions as a political tool to allow it to charge higher prices. The industry may even choose to locate research in the district of a powerful member of Congress because he or she may be able to arrange for the government to buy their drugs at patent-protected prices.[9]

The perverse incentives from patent monopolies affect other aspects of the research process, as well. Most of the research financed by the industry is not actually done in their own labs. Instead, it is farmed out to researchers, primarily those based at universities. In this case also, the industry has little incentive to try to minimize costs. A substantial portion of the money paid to university-based researchers is skimmed off by the universities, in some cases providing a substantial source of funding to these universities. By making universities dependent on their research money, the drug companies gain a powerful political ally in the battle for stronger patent protections. Many drug companies would gladly inflate their research bills in order to gain universities as allies in their battles.

The same logic applies to the other major component of research costs, clinical trials. Clinical trials are run by doctors – the people who decide what

---

[8]"The Campaign Against Innovation," International Federation of Pharmaceutical Manufacturers and Associations, [http://www.ifpma.org/News/SpeechDetail.aspx?nID=496].

[9] See "Drugmakers Win Exemption in House Budget-Cutting Bill," *Washington Post*, November 30, 2005.

drugs to prescribe to patients. The pharmaceutical industry spends tens of billions of dollars marketing its drugs to doctors. While it is illegal to pay doctors kickbacks to prescribe drugs, it would be virtually impossible to prosecute a drug company that buys a bit of goodwill by paying doctors more than is necessary to gain their participation in clinical trials.[10] The industry can expect to have these excess "research costs" repaid many times over in more prescriptions at patent-protected prices. In short, government patent monopolies lead to a predictable trend of ever more bloated research costs.

Alternatives to Patent Supported Prescription Drug Research

Patent monopolies might be a bad mechanism for financing prescription drug research, but we still need to find a way to pay for research, since the market by itself will not be sufficient. There are a number of different ways that research can be supported and in fact already is supported.[11] The federal government already spends more than $30 billion a year supporting bio-medical research, primarily through the National Institutes of Health (NIH). This spending has enjoyed widespread political support, especially from the pharmaceutical industry, which has vigorously pushed for increased spending over the last two decades. (Under the current system, NIH research is effectively a subsidy to the pharmaceutical industry.)

Most NIH funding supports basic research, but public money could be redirected towards the development and testing of new drugs. The government could double what it currently spends on research.[12] This money should be enough to replace the industry's patent supported research, since it wouldn't be wasted on copycat research or be used to buy political influence or to pay kickbacks to doctors for prescribing drugs. The research funded by the government would be made fully public upon completion and all patents based on publicly funded research would be placed in the public domain, so that all new drugs could be produced as generics in a competitive market.

To ensure that researchers have substantial incentives to do important work, it is possible to establish a substantial prize fund (e.g. $500 million a year) that could be used to give researchers who achieve extraordinary breakthroughs substantial rewards that would be in addition to their ordinary salaries. Many researchers could receive awards in the tens or hundreds of thousands of dollars for important discoveries. For truly extraordinary breakthroughs, researchers

---

[10] For example, see "As Doctors Write Prescriptions, Drug Company Writes a Check," *New York Times*, June 7, 2004.

[11] Baker (2004) lays out four alternatives to the patent system for supporting prescription drug research, including a variant of the method discussed in this section.

[12] It would probably be desirable to create a new structure outside of NIH to parcel out research dollars. The parceling out of research dollars could be done by private companies competing for long-term (e.g. 10-year) government contracts, with all companies subject to strict rules requiring openness for all research findings and that all patentable results be placed in the public domain.

could receive prizes in the millions of dollars, or even tens of millions, if their work leads to drugs that save or extend the lives of a large number of people.

This alternative to patent-financed drug research would in some respects require a smaller role for the government in the drug development process than the patent system. For example, the government would not have to micromanage the conduct of research by deciding when a drug, or even a research process, has infringed on another company's patent. It also would not have to arrest people for buying and selling drugs, as can be the case now when a person buys pills in a transaction that the patent holder claims it did not authorize.

This alternative system would likely also save consumers and even the government a substantial amount of money. The Center for Medicare and Medicaid Services (CMS) projects that the United States will spend $450 billion on drugs in 2015.[13] If these drugs were all available at generic prices, the cost would be approximately 70 percent less, a savings of $310 billion. CMS projects that the government will be spending $190 billion on prescription drugs in 2015. If it could save 70 percent on its prescription drug costs, this would amount to $130 billion in 2015. The government would still be ahead even if it will be spending $50 billion a year in prescription drug research at that point. Consumers would then be saving from both lower taxes and much lower drug prices.

Getting Beyond Nanny State Patent and Copyright Monopolies

Is the system described in the last section the best system for supporting prescription drug research? Is it better than the current patent system? Whether or not this is the best system, this is the debate that the public should be having on prescription drugs. The patent system for supporting prescription drug research is imposing too large a burden on the economy and public health for it to persist without question.

Similar questions should be raised about patent and copyright protections in other areas of the economy. Copyrights on computer software vastly increase the cost of computers, and make many software applications quite costly, when they could be transferred at no cost over the Internet. Can there be mechanisms for publicly financing software development that allow new software to be distributed cheaply or free? There would be enormous gains to the economy if software were freely available and the price of computers was no longer inflated by royalties on operating systems and applications. The savings from eliminating copyright and patent protection on software would be in the neighborhood of $70 billion to $100 billion a year.[14] In addition, the process of software development would almost certainly be more efficient if all software was placed in the public domain where anyone was free to work on it. As with publicly financed prescription drug research, a large body of public domain software

---

[13] These data are taken from the Center for Medicare and Medicaid Services (2006, Table 11).
[14] This estimate is derived in Baker (2005a).

54

would eliminate the incentive to make duplicative programs and applications that were not qualitatively better than existing programs and applications.

Textbooks present another situation in which the mechanism of copyright financed production does not seem to be leading to good results. Textbook prices have been rising at the rate of 6 percent a year since the late eighties, approximately 3 percentage points more rapidly that the overall rate of inflation. The incentives created by copyright monopolies encourage textbook publishers to constantly adapt their books to persuade faculty to use new editions, even when the research in the area provides little reason to change a textbook. This quickly makes used editions obsolete.

In addition, textbook publishers practice the same sort of price discrimination as pharmaceutical companies, charging lower prices in Europe and developing countries than they do in the United States. To preserve this type of price discrimination, the textbook publishers, like the drug companies, rely on the nanny state to police their marketing arrangements. They want the government to arrest people who sell their books at the wrong price in the wrong place, since large price differences cannot persist in a truly free market.

It would be a simple matter to establish a small pool of public money to contract with publishers to produce textbooks. As with prescription drugs, all the textbooks produced with public funds would be in the public domain and freely available over the Internet.[15] A pool of $300 million a year would be sufficient to produce 3,000 textbooks a year, assuming an average cost of $100,000 each. (Presumably, some textbooks would cost considerably more than $100,000 to produce, and some would cost less, depending on their length, subject matter, and quality.) Since all of these textbooks would be available over the Internet, college students could save the $12 billion they currently spend on textbooks, minus whatever amount they spend printing out segments of the books in hardcopy. This alternative mechanism would also have the benefit of allowing professors to mix and match sections from different textbooks, instead of being largely bound to rely on a single textbook for an entire course.

Of course, this alternative system could exist side-by-side with the existing copyright financed system. If professors felt that the publicly financed system was not producing worthwhile textbooks, then they would be free to assign a textbook supported by copyright, and sold at copyright protected prices, just as they do now.[16] There is no reason not to experiment with various paths. Certainly pluralistic solutions pose no problem for publicly financed research and creative work.

Using Vouchers to Combat Copyright Monopolies

When it comes to music, movies, books, and other forms of creative work, most of us do not want some government czar of culture and information

---

15 This sort of system is described in Baker (2005b).

16 In the same way, there is no reason that Pfizer, Merck, and other pharmaceutical companies could not continue to develop drugs supported through the patent system. They would just have to accept the risk that better drugs might be available at generic prices.

deciding what can be produced. This means that it is probably not desirable to have a centralized mechanism for allocating funds in these areas. Instead we can turn to a favorite tool of many conservatives: vouchers.

The basic principle is very simple. Suppose every adult were given a sum of money in the form of a tax voucher (e.g. $75) to support any form of creative or artistic work they like. The money can go to any person (singer, writer, musicians, movie director, etc.) or intermediary who registers to be eligible to receive the money.

The model on which this is based is the charitable tax deduction, where any religious, charitable, or non-profit organizations can receive tax deductible contributions, if they register with the Internal Revenue Service. As with the system of non-profit status, the government does not attempt to evaluate the quality of the work that the recipients do, it only intervenes to ensure that no fraud is being committed. The difference is that this contribution would be a voucher and the size would be small relative to what some individuals contribute to tax exempt organizations. The people who receive money through this "artistic freedom voucher (AFV)" system would be obligated to put all their work in the public domain.[17]

This AFV system would make an enormous amount of creative work available all over the world at no cost. If the voucher were set at $75 a person, and three quarters of the population chose to use their vouchers, it would generate more than $11 billion to support creative and artistic work. This would be sufficient to support more than 2 million creative/artistic workers at an average compensation of more than $50,000 a year.

In this case, too, the artistic freedom voucher system could compete side by side with the existing copyright system. If certain performers opted to rely on copyright protections rather than accept AFV money, they would be free to do so.[18] Similarly, if people opted to pay copyright-protected prices to buy copyrighted work, rather than obtaining it free over the Internet, they would have the option to do so.

Can Progressives Move Beyond the Middle Ages?

The alternatives outlined above may not be the best alternatives to patents and copyrights for supporting innovation and creative work. But that doesn't matter. The point is that there are alternative mechanisms to patents and copyrights that should be discussed. Patents and copyrights are relics of the Medieval guild system that are having increasingly negative consequences in the

---

[17] The sort of rules that would be needed for this system are discussed in more detail in Baker (2003).

[18] It would be necessary to have some restriction on creative workers receiving money from the AFV system and then gaining copyright protection – the purpose of the AFV system is not create a farm system where the best talent can be gleaned by the entertainment industry. For example, people receiving money through the AFV system can be prohibited from gaining copyright protection for 5 years afterwards. This system would be entirely self-enforcing, because it simply means that the copyright of anyone who violates the law is unenforceable.

21st century. In the case of patents, the most obvious negative consequence is denying lifesaving medicines to people who need them and could afford them if they were sold in a free market. It is also proving to be an increasingly inefficient mechanism for supporting drug research.

In the case of copyrights, the software and entertainment industry are pushing laws that require a growing role for the government in policing what people download on their computers and listen to on their iPods and cell phones. They have even had professors arrested for designing software algorithms and presenting their work at academic conferences.[19] Patents and copyrights might have been great institutions for the 16th century, but they don't work well in the 21st century. The alternatives outlined in this discussion are set out as examples of the mechanisms that could be used to support innovation and creative work. These proposals can be improved, or better ones developed.

Of course, the nanny state conservatives don't want anyone raising questions about patents and copyrights. They want to promote the conservative nanny state creationist myth that patents and copyrights are part of the natural order of things, or at least that the economy could not exist without them. They also don't want anyone to notice that in addition to being inefficient, patents and copyrights also have the effect of making some people, like Bill Gates, outrageously rich. While progressives may want to help Bill Gates in the same way that nanny state conservatives want to help needy mothers, there is only so much economic inefficiency we can tolerate. We need to develop more efficient mechanisms for the 21st century, and if one side effect is that the alternatives to patents and copyrights don't distribute income upward in the same way, most progressives will be able to live with that outcome.

---

[19] A Russian software programmer was indicted in 2001 after he gave a lecture at an academic conference explaining how a certain form of encryption could be broken "In the 'Idea Wars,' a Fight to Control a New Currency," *New York Times*, November 11, 2001.

CHAPTER FIVE

Mommy, Joey Owes Me Money

How Bankruptcy Laws are Bailing Out the Rich

In a free market economy, businesses know that investment decisions don't always work out as expected. Sometimes businesses invest in developing a product that turns out not to be as good as they believed, or that doesn't have the market they anticipated. They may invest based on trends, such as rising oil prices, that do not continue, leaving them with large losses. Or, they may extend credit to people, businesses, or countries that turn out to be bad credit risks. No one expects that the government will step in and sustain the demand for a bad product. Nor do we expect the government to intervene to make sure investors' expectations about rising oil prices are realized, for example, by buying up massive amounts of petroleum. But when it comes to making bad credit decisions, the nanny state conservatives do expect the government to step in and bail them out.

The nanny state conservatives think that it is the role of the government to act as a strong-arm debt collector for businesses that did not accurately assess the risks associated with their loans. This applies both nationally and internationally. They want the government to chase after individual debtors, following them throughout their lives, to wring out every possible cent of debt repayment. Internationally, they rely on the power of the International Monetary Fund to help them collect on bad loans. After all, huge multi-national banks can't be expected to understand credit risks in places like South Korea, Indonesia, or Argentina, that would be hard work. And, who needs to do hard work when the nanny state will come to the rescue?

Debt and Responsibility: The Two Sides of the Equation

When the nanny state conservatives wanted to stiffen the personal bankruptcy laws, they managed to effectively control the terms of the debate. They framed the issue as being a question of responsibility, in which people who had borrowed large amounts of money had an obligation to pay off their debts. The opponents of the measure were the bleeding hearts who pointed out that the vast majority of personal bankruptcies were the result of illness, job loss, and/or family breakup. They pointed out that the cases of people racking up huge bills on wild spending sprees or just straight out deadbeats who were trying to evade their debts were exceptions, not the typical bankruptcy case.[1]

Of course, it is reasonable to ask about the circumstances that push people into bankruptcy before taking steps to impose harsher bankruptcy rules, but it is

---

[1] For a discussion of the importance of illness as a factor in bankruptcy, see Himmelstein et al. (2005).

also reasonable to ask about the creditors who lend the money. The banks, credit companies, and other financial institutions supposedly make their profit by being able to accurately assess credit risk. That is the whole story of being a financial intermediary. Savers put money in a checking or money market account, buy a CD, or lend money in some other form to a bank or other financial institution, which then turns around and lends the money at a higher rate of interest to a business or individual who wants to borrow.

The bank gets a higher rate of interest on its loans than the people who deposit money in its accounts because it is supposed to know what it is doing when making loans, whereas most of its depositors have no expertise in this area. If it turns out that everyone is defaulting on loans from banks and credit card companies, it is evidence that they are not effective in recognizing bad credit risks. In a market economy, we should want lenders with bad judgment to go out of business. After all, if these lenders can't distinguish good credit risks from bad credit risks, then it is bad for the economy and bad for society that they stay in business. It means that credit is not going to the best possible uses.

But instead of having the incompetent lenders go out of business (actually most banks weren't worried about going out of business, they just wanted higher profits), the conservative nanny state stepped in to bail them out with the 2005 bankruptcy law, using the force of the government to squeeze every last cent from debtors. Under the new bankruptcy laws, the government will monitor debtors for many years after they have declared bankruptcy, seizing assets or garnishing wages for debts that may have been incurred 20 or 30 years in the past. This might sound like a tall order, but when big banks are troubled, the nanny state is there to help.

The fact that the new bankruptcy laws were actually increasing the role of the government in the economy was largely missing from the debate. Historically, most loans required little involvement from the government because they were attached to physical property such as land, a house, or a car. If a debtor had fallen behind on his payments, then the role of the court in the debt collection process was essentially a one-time proposition: the court would simply require the debtor to turn over ownership of the relevant asset to the creditor, and the case would be over. The provisions of the new bankruptcy laws essentially mean that the courts could be following a debtor for the rest of his life, if he has not paid off his debts.

However, in the last two decades there has been an explosion of debt, mostly credit card debt, that is not secured by a physical asset. At the beginning of 1980, the outstanding value of "revolving credit" (a category that is mostly composed of credit card debt) was just over $120 billion. By the beginning of 2006, revolving credit had grown to more than $800 billion (both numbers in 2006 dollars).[2] The growth of this form of credit is not necessarily a bad thing. Many people find themselves in need of loans to get through hard times or to

---

[2] This data is taken from the Federal Reserve Board's Consumer Credit series, which is available on its website at [http://content.healthaffairs.org/cgi/content/abstract/hlthaff.w5.63v1]. (Nominal stocks of debt were deflated with the CPI-URS).

make important purchases before they earn the money to pay for them. But, the mere fact that this form of debt grew so rapidly shows that the risk of default on these loans was not a serious obstacle to credit card lending or other forms of unattached loans. Tens of millions of people were having no trouble getting access to loans through credit cards or other types of credit.

There is an argument that consumers will benefit if the risk of default on credit cards and other debt is made lower as the result of tighter bankruptcy laws. In principle, lower default rates should lead to lower interest rates for borrowers, since credit card companies have to charge an interest rate high enough to offset the losses from loans that are never paid off. The extent to which borrowers will ever see a bankruptcy dividend in the form of lower interest rates is questionable, but even if increased debt collection does lead to lower credit card interest rates, there are still costs associated with the increased role for the government under the new bankruptcy law.[3]

The effect of the government's increased role in debt collection is largely the same as the effect of an increase in taxes. If workers know that a large portion of their wages, for example, 15 percent, will be pulled out of their paychecks and sent to their creditors, then it has the same effect on their incentive to work as if the government were pulling another 15 percentage points out of their paycheck in taxes. The nanny state conservatives know very well how much economic harm is done by high taxes. The same amount of harm is done when the "tax" is a payment to creditors from the distant past. The result is that workers will have less incentive to work because they keep a smaller chunk of their paycheck.

Perhaps more importantly, since few people really have the option of not working, workers with large debt burdens will have more incentive to work off the books, doing odd jobs or earning income in other ways that is not being reported to the government. In other contexts, conservatives have viewed this as a bad outcome.

As a practical matter, the enhanced debt collection structure put in place through the bankruptcy reform bill passed in 2005 is likely to have other undesirable consequences, the most important of which might be reduced child support collection. In principle, child support payments still have priority over repayment of debts, so that creditors can only get repayment from money left over after all child support has been paid. However, money cannot be strictly separated in this way. If debt repayments prevent a non-custodial father from

---

[3] There have been several papers examining the weak link between credit card interest rates and other interest rates in the economy. The research suggests that banks tend not to pass on lower costs of funds in the form of lower interest rates to borrowers because they do not want to compete directly on the basis of low interest rates. The reason is that the people who select credit cards primarily based on the interest rates they charge are the ones who are most likely to default, and therefore are not customers that the credit card issuers really want (see Calem and Mester, 1995). Insofar as this explanation is correct, consumers are likely to see little benefit in the form of lower interest rates, even if the new bankruptcy law succeeds in substantially reducing default rates.

ever accumulating money in a bank account, and the father loses his job, then the child support payments will stop as soon as the paychecks stop.

Similarly, if this father decides to work off the books in order to evade debt repayment, it will be much harder for the government to track his income in order to force him to make child support payments. We will only know how much of an impact the bankruptcy law has on child support payments in a few years, but protecting the flow of child support does not appear to have been a major consideration in the design of the bill.

There is another important weakness in the logic behind the bankruptcy reform bill – there is no rationale for making it apply to debts already incurred. If we believe that consumers will benefit from lower interest rates on loans because the new bankruptcy bill lowers the risk of default, then this is a reasonable argument for the new bankruptcy law, even if it means a stronger role for the government in the economy. But the reduction in default risk can only change the interest rate on loans that consumers take out in the *future*. Banks and credit companies are not going to reduce the interest rate on loans they have already issued because the tougher bankruptcy law means that the default rate on these loans will be lower than under the old law. Any reduction in the default rate in prior loans is pure profit for the credit card industry and other creditors.

In effect, the conservative nanny state has rewritten the terms of these loans after the fact in a way that benefits creditors. Borrowers took out loans under one set of bankruptcy rules. The lenders also willingly made these loans under the old bankruptcy rules. Presumably, the lenders understood the risk of default that was implied given the bankruptcy law in place at the time. Then the financial industry got the nanny state to change the rules in a way that not only applied to future loans, but also to the ones that were already issued. (The law could have been written to only apply to debts incurred after its date of passage, with the old bankruptcy rules continuing to apply to pre-existing debt.) In this way, the nanny state gave a huge gift to the financial industry at the expense of debtors.

However, it would be wrong to say that the conservative nanny state is always hostile to debtors. The new bankruptcy law included a provision that allowed three states (Florida, Kansas, and Texas) to retain a homestead exemption in their state bankruptcy laws. This exemption allows a person who goes bankrupt to shield as much money as they want from creditors in the form of equity in their homes. In some cases, the amount that is protected could run into millions of dollars.

This could mean, for example, that if a contractor did $100,000 of repair work on the home of a Hollywood actor, and the actor chose to declare bankruptcy rather than pay the bill, the contractor would simply be out of luck. This would be the case even if the actor's home was worth $10 million. By contrast, if a renter owed a hospital $100,000 for an operation, she would not be able to shield even $10,000 in a bank account. Obviously, the conservative nanny state likes homeowners and doesn't like renters. It will protect you from your creditors if you decide to buy a house, and it will help your creditors hound you to your grave if you rent.

The International Monetary Fund: The Nanny State Goes Overseas

The conservative nanny state doesn't just help creditors here at home, it also offers a helping hand internationally. When big U.S. financial institutions look for investment opportunities elsewhere in the world, they don't go alone. If their investments turn out poorly, U.S. banks can look to a helping hand from the International Monetary Fund (IMF), which tries to ensure that foreign debtors don't stiff the big multi-national banks.

The IMF is a holdover from a different era. It was initially established in 1945 to sustain the system of fixed exchange rates put in place at the end of World War II. Under this system, the U.S. dollar was supposed to be the key currency, with all countries fixing the value of their currency to it and the value of the dollar, in turn, tied to gold. The role of the IMF in this system was to provide credit for countries that were having temporary difficulty supporting their exchange rate. This could happen if a country had a problem with inflation or a large trade deficit, both of which could cause people to dump a currency. The IMF was supposed to lend money to a country to allow it to sustain the value of its currency while it made the adjustments necessary to correct the initial problem.

The IMF filled this role until the collapse of the Bretton Woods system of fixed exchange rates in 1973. The problem with the system was that the United States, the country with the key currency, had itself begun to have problems supporting its currency. In 1971, The United States was able to arrange for a reduction in the value of the dollar against both gold and the other currencies in the world. When another adjustment became necessary in 1973, it proved easier to simply scrap the fixed exchange rate system rather than go back to negotiate another round of devaluations of the dollar. With the end of the fixed exchange rate system, the IMF lost the purpose for which it had originally been designed.

As free market conservatives know, government bureaucracies rarely go out of business, even if the reason for their existence has disappeared. Following the tradition of bureaucracies everywhere, the IMF found itself a new purpose following the collapse of the Bretton Woods system. It became an international debt collector. Whenever countries fell into crises and found themselves unable to repay loans to western creditors, the IMF stepped in to assure the largest possible debt repayment.

The way in which the IMF performed this function was to effectively make itself the agent of an international creditors' cartel. This role is important in the context of a country facing an economic crisis. In the absence of an agency like the IMF, the normal force of market pressures would lead each creditor to rush to cut its own deal, while the country still had some money to pay out. This could mean that creditors would take large losses – perhaps accepting payments that are just a small fraction of the money owed – because they fear that if they wait before reaching a deal, the terms will be worse, since most of the money will already be gone. With each deal that gets made, the country has less money to pay off the remaining creditors, so in the absence of any international coordination mechanism, there would be a rush to make a quick deal with a country in crisis, even if it was necessary to write off most of its debt as a loss.

In its role as an agent of the creditors' cartel, the IMF is there to block the rush to the exit that is dictated by market forces. The IMF negotiates collectively on behalf of creditors. It can impose conditions on a country in crisis that are designed to maximize the amount of money that can be repaid to its creditors. Often these conditions are politically unpopular in the country suffering a crisis, since they can involve large cuts in public services and/or increases in taxes. For most governments, especially ones that have to run in democratic elections, the option of defaulting on debts to foreign creditors is more appealing than major cuts in public services and large tax increases.

However, the IMF can exert substantial weight on behalf of the foreign creditors. The IMF will refuse to make additional loans to a government that does not come to an agreement with it on dealing with foreign creditors. Failure to reach agreement with the IMF typically cuts off access to loans from the World Bank as well, which lends approximately three times as much money as the IMF.

Even more important than losing access to credit from the international financial institutions is the prospect of losing access to private credit markets. Until recently, failure to reach an agreement with the IMF would cut a country off from access to most bank loans and other normal forms of credit. For most developing countries, the loss of access to foreign sources of credit would halt normal trading patterns and threaten an economic collapse. The IMF's terms for reaching an agreement, however harsh, might look very good in comparison.[4]

In the last quarter century the IMF has imposed programs on dozens of countries throughout the developing world. In many cases, the result has been a sustained period of little or no growth. This is seen most clearly in Latin America. Per capita GDP in the region had increased by more than 80 percent over the two decades from 1960 to 1980. After most of the countries in the region found themselves in serious debt problems at the beginning of the eighties, they were forced to follow a different economic course. As a result, per capita GDP has risen by little more than 10 percent in the last quarter century. While IMF-imposed policies don't completely explain the entire growth slowdown, it is reasonable to believe that they were part of the story. The IMF

---

[4] The ability of the IMF to impose conditions has been substantially reduced by several recent trends. First, most developing countries are now net exporters of capital when their debt service is factored into the equation. This means that if a country loses all access to foreign credit, but also stops making debt service payments, it is actually on net better off. This is the reason that Argentina was able to refuse the IMF's terms after its default in 2001. Its economy has boomed even as it has unilaterally written off the bulk of Argentina's foreign debt. China, the world's largest exporter of capital, also creates a huge source of funds that is not necessarily under the IMF's control. If China opts to make loans to a country that has not come to terms with the IMF, then it can readily replace any capital flows that the IMF would have made available.

has forced countries to pay a serious price in order to maximize their debt repayment to creditors.

The IMF's nanny state intervention in the market is offensive, not only because it works to benefit many of the largest and ostensibly most sophisticated investors at the expense of the world's poor, but also because it ignores the fact that these investors were already compensated for their risk. When countries face an economic crisis, the market responds by raising the interest rate on loans to those countries. For example, as Argentina's financial crisis was building in 1999-2001, the real interest rate (which is adjusted for the effect of inflation) was hovering near 20 percent. The reason why loans carried 20 percent real interest rates in Argentina, compared to 1 to 2 percent in the United States, is because investors understood that there were large risks associated with loans to Argentina.

If the IMF comes in after the fact to ensure that Argentina pays off its loans (as it tried to do, unsuccessfully) it is, in effect, handing a windfall to investors at the expense of Argentina's people. Informed investors understood they were taking a risk when they invested in Argentina, which is why they were getting such a high rate of interest on their loans. It turns out that they lost their bet, because Argentina defaulted. The market response should have been that the banks that judged risk poorly take a financial hit, and the particular individuals who exercised bad judgment on loans should perhaps lose their jobs. In a free market, there is no place for a supranational institutional like the IMF to rewrite the rules to ensure that creditors are protected.

The IMF provided the same sort of service in the East Asian financial crisis in the fall of 1997. In that situation, the IMF forced governments in the region to assume the responsibility to repay loans that banks made to private companies. The problem facing the foreign banks was that these countries had no well-developed bankruptcy laws, so there was no mechanism through which foreign banks could collect on loans made to companies that were essentially bankrupt at the time. The IMF came to the rescue by requiring that governments repay these debts before they would be allowed normal access to credit markets.[5]

In a Free Market, Lenders Take Risks

Much of the national debate over bankruptcy laws and the international debate over the role of the IMF has been permeated with comments about the need for responsibility and the moral obligation to repay debts. People can arrive at their own moral judgments, but in a market economy lenders take risks when they make a loan. They should, in principle, understand this fact. Certainly, the highly compensated corporate executives that manage large banks and other financial institutions should understand that they take risks when they make their loans. When the government takes the role of a strong-arm debt collector, especially on loans that were made in the past under different rules, it

---

[5] This bailout is discussed in Goldstein (1998).

intervenes on behalf of the creditor, at the expense of the debtor. This conservative nanny state intervention should never be confused with the free market.

CHAPTER SIX

The Rigged Legal Deck

Torts and Takings (The Nanny State Only Gives)

In recent years, the nanny state conservatives have taken aim at the country's legal system. One of the arch-villains in their mythology is the trial lawyer. According to the nanny state conservatives, trial lawyers can make 12 otherwise reasonable people award ridiculous amounts of money in damages when they sit on a jury in a court case. In the conservative nanny state mythology, activist judges are their accomplices, allowing trial lawyers to inflict harm on the productive segments of society.

In fact, the nanny state conservatives are so concerned about the extraordinary power that trial lawyers can use to influence juries (as distinct from the power that Madison Avenue marketing wizards might wield over consumers or voters) that they want the nanny state to rein them in. The nanny state conservatives want the government to sharply limit the amount of damages that these crazed juries can award. They also want the government to restrict the types of contracts that plaintiffs can sign with lawyers. The nanny state conservatives apparently believe that in a free market, there might be too much incentive to sue corporations, doctors, and other wealthy people for damages. Proponents of free markets might expect that individuals and corporations should be accountable for the damages they cause. But the nanny state conservatives believe that the government should intervene to prevent the wealthy from being held too accountable.

The Nanny State Conservative's Myth of the Broken Legal System

The nanny state conservatives illustrate the problem of the U.S. legal system with a collection of horror stories. Probably the most famous is the one about the elderly woman who won millions of dollars from McDonald's after she burned herself by spilling hot McDonald's coffee in her lap while driving. A close second is the story about the would-be burglar who broke his neck by falling through a skylight, and then won millions of dollars from the homeowner in damages.

The lesson the nanny state conservatives would have us take from these stories is that the legal system is out of control. Juries award ridiculous sums in cases involving little if any real harm to individuals, or at least none that can legitimately be blamed on the defendants. As a result, the defendants are powerless against the trial lawyers. Defendants need the helping hand of the nanny state in order to prevent the trial lawyers from using juries to take all their money.

This is the essence of so-called "tort reform." The tort reformers want the government to put caps on the size of damages that can be awarded in various cases. They also want the government to prohibit certain types of contracts between plaintiffs and their attorneys. For example, some tort reform proposals limit the percentage of the jury award that the lawyer can receive in a contingency fee. Apparently, the nanny state conservatives don't trust individuals to decide for themselves what sort of contracts they should sign with their lawyers. The full list of proposals that have appeared under the guise of "tort reform" is long and complicated, but the basic point is that the nanny state conservatives who support these measures believe that the government must intervene in the legal system to prevent defendants (who are usually relatively wealthy) from being held fully accountable for the harm that they have done.

The Legal Myths: A Closer Look

The legal horror stories from the nanny state conservatives make a compelling case, but the reality isn't quite the same as the myth. A key fact in the McDonald's coffee case is that McDonald's served especially hot coffee because the heat concealed the taste. This allowed them to use a cheaper brand of coffee, thereby increasing profits. The elderly woman, who suffered third degree burns, was not the first person who had complained after being scalded by McDonald's coffee. In fact, McDonald's received hundreds of letters from people who had been burnt by their coffee. In addition, although the jury did award the woman $2.9 million, this sum was reduced by the trial judge, and then reduced further to $600,000 in a settlement as the case was being appealed.[1]

The would-be burglar case is more difficult to track down. In a case that may fit the bill, the "burglar" was a high school student who was crawling around on the roof of his school with his friends. The skylight that he fell through was painted the same color as the roof, which made it difficult to recognize as a skylight. There had been two prior instances in which students had fallen through the skylight, but the school did nothing to address the problem. The student who won the suit was paralyzed for life.

One can disagree with these verdicts, but the actual cases are less outrageous than the fables told by nanny state conservatives. The differences are important. First, when juries do act unreasonably, presumably sane judges (the vast majority of sitting judges in the United States were appointed by Republicans) have the power to unilaterally reduce the verdict. And they often use this power. Furthermore, excessive verdicts can be whittled down on appeal, as happened in the McDonald's case. The likelihood that 12 otherwise normal people will issue a loony verdict and get it past a judge and through the appellate process is very small, even when they act under the evil influence of trial lawyers.

Punitive Damages and Private Law Enforcement

There is another important aspect to these stories that the nanny state conservatives would prefer the public overlook. The damages awarded in these

---

[1] An account of this case can be found in Burke (2002, pp. 28-29).

cases, and many others like them, are not intended merely to compensate the people who had brought the suits, they are also intended to punish the defendants for what the juries viewed as bad behavior. The jury felt that McDonald's had been wrong to risk burning customers by making their coffee unusually hot so that the company could save a fraction of a penny on every cup. They were not simply thinking of how to compensate the woman who was burned, they wanted to teach McDonald's a lesson that would get them to change their practices.[2]

Similarly, the jury that awarded damages to the injured student wanted to send a message to this particular school and others like it. Having skylights painted the same color as the roof posed an obvious hazard, which should have been apparent to the school since two students had previously fallen through the skylights, apparently without serious injuries. The school could have taken reasonable precautions, like painting the skylights a different color. While climbing on the roof might have been against the law, it was reasonable to believe that adolescent boys would do it. Since the school apparently lacked the ability to keep its students from climbing on the roof, it could have taken precautions to ensure that the roof was not unnecessarily dangerous. In this case, the jury effectively warned schools that they should expect that their students will sometimes break the rules, and that they should take reasonable precautions to prevent them from becoming injured when they do.

In bringing cases like these, the plaintiffs are not only helping themselves if they collect damages, they are actually performing a public service, by punishing individuals, corporations, or governments for acting irresponsibly. Large settlements in these cases discourage others from acting irresponsibly in the same way, just as a large fine from the government might send a message.

The punitive aspect of these settlements is important to understand because that is precisely the reason that punitive damages are allowed in many cases. Dealing with gross negligence through the legal system is sometimes referred to as "private law enforcement," because the act of filing a suit replaces the function of a government regulatory agency. The argument that it might be desirable to have private individuals rather than the government impose sanctions through the courts has actually been put forward by some prominent conservative legal scholars – most notably Richard Posner, a University of Chicago law professor and Reagan appointee to the appellate court. These scholars have argued for the merits of private law enforcement as a deterrent to harmful behavior.[3] This approach can imply a smaller role for government, not a bigger one, unless of course the intention is that corporations and individuals not be held accountable for the harm they cause.

---

[2] The verdict accomplished this goal. McDonald's no longer serves super-heated coffee.
[3] For a discussion of private law enforcement as a means of discouraging harmful behavior, see Posner (1986, pp. 562-566).

Limiting Legal Fees and Contracts

The tort reformers want the public to believe that they are clamping down on trial lawyers when they propose limits on the fees that lawyers can collect in a settlement. In reality, they are trying to make it more difficult to sue by making it more difficult to hire a lawyer.

Winning a legal suit against a major corporation is a long and expensive process, even when a plaintiff has a solid case. A major corporation will be represented by lawyers who have the time and experience to make advancing a case as difficult as possible. At the first step, most lawsuits involve a phase of discovery, a fact-finding process where both sides try to gather evidence to use at trial. A corporate defendant can make this process time-consuming and expensive for the plaintiff by refusing requests for evidence and forcing the plaintiff's lawyer to repeatedly ask a judge to order a disclosure. It is standard practice for corporate lawyers to drag out the discovery process as long as possible.

After the discovery process, the corporation will routinely ask that a lawsuit be dismissed on summary judgment – essentially have the judge say that there is no basis for a lawsuit – so that there is no trial and a jury would never hear the case. Even if a plaintiff gets past summary judgment, the lawyer has likely been forced to spend a great deal of time preparing the case. A corporation can raise almost any issue it wants as a basis for summary judgment, and a plaintiff's lawyer will have to respond to each issue or risk having a suit dismissed on trivial grounds.

If a suit survives summary judgment, then both sides prepare for trial. Here, too, there are opportunities for delays as corporate lawyers can contest what items can be accepted as evidence and which witnesses can be brought into the trial to testify. Each time that the corporate lawyers make a motion, the plaintiff's lawyers must argue against it, no matter how weak the defendant's argument may be.

In the event that the plaintiff wins a verdict from the jury, the corporate lawyers will routinely ask the judge to either overturn the verdict or reduce the amount that the jury awarded. If the judge allows the verdict to stand and does not substantially reduce the size of the settlement, the corporate lawyers will almost invariably appeal the verdict. While the odds of having a verdict overturned on appeal are low, the process can delay any payment by several years. Often plaintiffs negotiate a settlement for a sum substantially less than the jury's award in order to avoid the delay and uncertainty associated with the appeals.

Most cases never advance to the point of reaching a jury. A recent study by the Congressional Budget Office (2003) found that only 3 percent of tort suits were decided at trial. The verdicts were roughly evenly split between plaintiffs and defendants. If a case actually goes to trial, the process will usually take years, even prior to any appeals. During this period, a lawyer working on a contingency basis will receive no payment, and if the case is dismissed at any point prior to trial or the plaintiff loses at trial, the plaintiff's lawyer will receive nothing.

These facts are important in the context of proposals to limit legal fees, because in most cases, plaintiffs' lawyers collect no fees if they take a case on a straight contingency basis. This means that the relatively small percentage of cases that they win must also compensate them for the time spent on cases for which they were not paid. If a lawyer considering a long and potentially complicated case could not charge a high fee, he or she would likely refuse the case, or refuse to take it on a contingency basis. This means that unless the plaintiff was able to pay the lawyers' fee in advance (which few people could afford), then they would not be able to get a lawyer to take the case.

In short, this is the point of the tort reformers' efforts to restrict legal fees for plaintiffs' lawyers – they don't propose restrictions on how much money corporate lawyers can be paid. They want to make the probability of winning sufficiently low, and the eventual payout sufficiently small, so that few lawyers will want to take a lawsuit against a major corporation. Price controls on lawyers' fees have no place in a free market. In a free market people can sign any contract they want with a lawyer, so this is a clear case of the nanny state coming to the rescue of defendants in civil cases.

The same logic applies to limits on punitive damages. If the limits are low, then the potential payout to people harmed by a corporation or doctor will be small. This means that in many cases, people who have been harmed will have little incentive to file a suit. This doesn't just affect the people who have been harmed. In a situation like the McDonald's coffee case, the suit forced McDonald's to change its policy of superheating coffee. This was an outcome that benefited the larger public, not just the woman who been burnt. If there was no possibility of punitive damages in this case, the suit probably would not have been brought, and McDonald's never would have changed its policy, and more people would have been injured.[4]

Of course this is precisely the goal of the nanny state conservatives. They don't want wealthy individuals and big corporations to be held accountable for the damage they cause. If they can make it difficult for victims to hire lawyers, and reduce the size of the compensation even when a plaintiff wins a case, then the wealthy and big corporations will be better able to inflict damage with impunity.

Beating Up on Lawyers the Right Way

The above discussion should not be taken to mean that there are not real cases of abuse of the U.S. legal system. There are plenty of unethical lawyers who press phony claims against doctors, small business owners, and major corporations. Measures that curb these abuses are a benefit to society. But the

---

[4] In several states, awards of punitive damages are shared with the government. This creates a situation in which private individuals still have an incentive to sue in cases where a corporation or individual has acted in a grossly irresponsible way, but they don't walk away with quite the same bonanza if they are able to prove this case in a trial.

nanny state conservatives seem more interested in obstructing real cases than weeding out phony ones. They also hugely exaggerate the size of the problem of bogus lawsuits.[5]

One obvious way to reduce the burden of lawsuits on society would be to reduce the costs of hiring lawyers. (It would also be desirable to eliminate many of the arcane legal rules that drive up costs.) The most obvious way that this could be done would be to standardize licensing requirements for practicing law nationwide and to open the door to foreign lawyers who met these standards. A modest influx of foreign lawyers (e.g. 20,000 a year – approximately 1.5 percent of annual immigration) could drastically reduce the cost of hiring of lawyers, saving consumers and the economy tens of billions of dollars a year.

There are also a wide variety of legal rules that serve little purpose, but do raise costs. These range from restrictions on the type and form of documents that can be filed with the court to notarizing signatures. If legal rules could be standardized across states, and unnecessary rules eliminated, it could further reduce the cost of the legal system.

There certainly have been cases in which lawyers' fees reach outlandish levels. The settlements in lawsuits by state governments against the tobacco industry awarded lawyers fees reaching into the billions of dollars in some instances. While this may be viewed as excessive, the cause of the problem is simple: incompetent public officials who signed bad contracts. While it is standard for lawyers to sign contracts that give them a share of settlements, there is no reason that the state officials who signed these contracts could not have imposed a limit on the size of fees. Potential fees could have been capped at some amount (say, $100 million) or, alternatively, there could have been a fee structure where the share of the settlement that went to lawyers was reduced at very high levels (e.g. the contingency fee falls to 20 percent for settlements between $500 million and $800 million, to 10 percent for settlements over $800 million, etc.). If state officials had used reasonable judgment in the contracts they offered in the tobacco cases, there would not have been an issue of excessive legal fees.

Takings: The Conservative Nanny State Only Gives

In recent years nanny state conservatives have made a major issue out of "takings," laws and regulations that reduce the value of private property. The issue of takings comes up often, but not exclusively, in the context of environmental regulation. For example, if the government prohibits building in a forest because it threatens the habitat of an endangered species, this usually reduces the value of the land. Similarly, in an effort to protect wetlands, the

---

[5] For example, a recent study found that the cost of defending medical malpractice cases in the United States was less than 0.5 percent of total health care spending. This figure was comparable to the costs in England, New Zealand, and Australia, all countries with much lower total health care expenditures, see Anderson et al. (2005).

federal government has placed restrictions on the uses of land in some areas. This could also reduce the value of the land.[6]

The nanny state conservatives argue that these government actions amount to an unlawful taking of property. They argue that if the government imposes regulations that reduce the value of private property, it should compensate the property owner for any loss incurred. This "no takings without compensation" demand was one of the rallying cries of the Republicans when they took control of Congress in 1994.

On its face, the demand seems to reflect simple fairness. After all, if the government decides that it is in the public interest to protect a particular species or habitat, why should the property owner who is having the use of her property restricted be the one to suffer? It's a good story, but at best it is only half of the story.

The government is constantly taking action that affects the value of private property. In some cases, like the ones noted above, its action can reduce the value of property, but at least as frequently governmental actions increase the value of private property. The most obvious situation in which government action increases the value of private property is when it improves the transportation infrastructure that makes a particular area more accessible by land or air transportation.

In the 19th century, farmland was of relatively little value, if there was no easy way to bring the output to market. In this context, building railroads, which came with huge government subsidies, could substantially increase the value of land. In recent years, the decision to locate a major highway in an area increased the value of land because it became accessible for suburban development. Locating a mass transit stop can have a similar effect. Building bridges to areas that had previously relied on ferry transportation also has an effect on land values, as does the construction of major airports that can accommodate large jets.

There are other ways in which government actions can significantly increase land values. Establishing a national park or other major tourist site can substantially increase the value of nearby land. Similarly, government regulations that clean lakes, rivers, harbors, or bays will also increase the value of nearby land.

The government also takes actions that increase the value of land that go beyond those that merely affect the physical features. People are willing to pay more for a house in a neighborhood with good public schools. This means that

---

[6] Examples of "takings" that have nothing to do with environmental protection are the construction of an airport, which is likely to substantially reduce the value of residential property in the immediate area, or placing a nuclear or hazardous waste dump in a particular area, which is also likely to depress land values. The takings issue has most often been associated with measures intended to protect the environment, but the uncompensated loss of property value due to governmental action is probably at least as common in the context of measures that are intended to promote economic growth.

if the government improves the schools in an area it also increases the land value. The same is true of measures that have the effect of reducing crime.

In short, there is a long list of actions that the government routinely undertakes that can substantially increase the value of the land in a specific area. In none of these cases does the government demand a check from landowners demanding compensation for the increase in their property value.[7] What the nanny state conservatives apparently want is a world in which the government must pay them any time they get harmed by its actions, but they get to keep the dividends of any benefits they derive from the government's action.

In fact, the idea of involving the courts every time that a government action lowers or increases the value of property is antithetical to the idea of leaving things to the market. If this approach were applied literally, the courts would be involved in almost any action the government took. When the government builds a highway in one area, it may increase property value for nearby land, but it reduces property values in other towns that might have hoped to be the site for the highway. Even reducing crime in one neighborhood, by having the effect of making other areas relatively more crime prone (if the crime rate in one neighborhood falls, and it stays constant in other neighborhoods, then the other neighborhoods have seen a rise in their relative crime rate) can be seen as having a negative impact on property values for some people. Taken to an extreme, the takings doctrine is not a free market doctrine. It would have the courts deciding almost everything.

As a practical matter, most government actions, either beneficial or harmful to property values, are not complete surprises. Landowners might know that the state government could build a highway in a specific area and therefore incorporate this expectation in the price that they are willing to pay for a plot of land. Similarly, landowners should recognize the possibility that environmental regulation can limit some uses of their land, which should also affect the price. In a market economy, we expect people to be intelligent and forward looking in their actions. If they did not anticipate a likely government action, why should the government bail them out because of their poor judgment?

Reasonable Rules on Takings

In most states, the rule that the courts apply on takings is that cases can only be brought in situations where the taking was nearly total; in effect, that the government had confiscated property. This is a standard that people who want to minimize the government's involvement in the economy should applaud. This standard avoids having the courts constantly intervene in the economy. It

---

[7] Some of the increase in property value may be captured in higher property taxes, but this would only be a small portion of the value, at least for the biggest gainers. It is also worth noting that the gains and losses in property values should be largely symmetrical in this respect. If gains in property value due to government action are retaken through higher property taxes, then any losses should largely be offset by lower property taxes, which would mean that taking really should not be an issue.

also encourages property owners to use good judgment in assessing the risk of government action when they buy property. This is the sort of personal responsibility that conservatives applaud in other contexts.

CHAPTER SEVEN

Small Business Babies

The vast majority of small business owners in the United States are honest hard-working people who are trying to make a better life for their children than the one they have. This is also true of the people who work as dishwashers, housekeepers, and custodians. The big difference between the two groups is that small business owners earn more money, on average, than dishwashers, housekeepers, and custodians, and they hold a more favored spot in conservative nanny state mythology. As a result, small business owners can count on a wide range of special benefits from the government, including low interest loans, special tax breaks, and exemptions from a wide range of health and safety regulations that are intended to protect workers, consumers, and the environment.

Small business owners earn this generosity by serving as an important prop for the conservative nanny state. There are a wide range of public policies that are defended or opposed based on their impact on small businesses. For example, in the 2004 presidential campaign, President Bush repeatedly defended the portion of the tax cuts that went to upper income taxpayers by claiming that these tax cuts benefited hundreds of thousands of small business owners.[1] Focus groups apparently showed that a tax cut that benefited people who owned small businesses sounded more appealing than a tax cut that just benefited wealthy people.

A few years earlier, Congress approved the repeal of the estate tax. One of the main arguments used by proponents of repeal was that the estate tax was forcing many heirs to sell off their family business in order to pay the tax. Given the high exemptions in the law, and special provisions allowing delayed payments for family businesses, it seemed unlikely that the estate tax was posing a serious problem to heirs who actually wanted to continue operating the family business.[2] Again, focus groups no doubt showed that preserving family owned

---

[1] This claim turned out to be a considerable stretch, as is often the case when making claims about small businesses. Many of the "small businesses" that benefited from the reduction in tax rates for higher income taxpayers were in fact partnerships that existed primarily as tax shelters, see Friedman (2004).

[2] The law allows the owner of a family business to pay out any taxes owed under the estate tax over a 14-year period, with no penalty. Much of the concern about families losing businesses due to the estate tax is the result of the difficulty that the public (and the media) have in distinguishing a marginal tax from an average tax. There is a large zero bracket for the estate tax, which exempted 98 percent of estates from the tax even before the phased repeal was approved by Congress in 2001. However, even when an estate crosses this threshold so that it is subject to the tax, it is only the amount *over* the threshold that is subject to the tax. For example, if the threshold is $1 million, and an estate is worth $1,050,000, then $50,000 of the estate is subject to tax, not the full $1,050,000. While a successful small business may creep over this threshold, the resulting tax (in this example, $8,500, based on a 17 percent tax rate) is likely to be small relative to the size of the estate. Any family interested in keeping a business worth

businesses through generations had more appeal to voters than saying that wealthy people didn't want their children to be taxed on their inheritance.

Of course, in reality the battle over the estate tax is an issue that is almost exclusively about wealthy people who don't want wealthy children to be taxed on their inheritance. In the spring of 2001 a *New York Times* reporter called the American Farm Bureau, one of the main groups lobbying for repeal of the estate tax, and asked to speak to a family that had lost its farm due to the estate tax. The Farm Bureau was unable to identify a single family in the entire country who had been through this experience.[3]

Small businesses do more than provide a cover for policies that redistribute income upward. Small business owners, like highly paid professionals, provide an important political base for conservative nanny state policies. For these reasons, they earn the benefits that the conservative nanny state confers on them.

Small Businesses and the Economy: Compelling Myth and Unpleasant Realities

Politicians of both parties are anxious to tout the virtues of small businesses, leaving few people willing to question, or even call attention to, the various benefits that the conservative nanny state bestows on them. For example, in his first State of the Union address, President Clinton touted the importance of small business as he announced his plans for a special small business investment tax credit. He cited a true but misleading fact: small businesses are responsible for the vast majority of job creation in the United States.

The fact is misleading because small businesses are also responsible for the vast majority of job destruction in the United States.[4] The U.S. economy involves an enormous amount of job churning, with 3 to 4 million workers getting jobs every month, and roughly 3 to 4 million workers leaving or losing jobs every month. Most of this churning takes place at small businesses, some of which add jobs as a result of being newly formed or growing. Other small businesses are forced to shed workers, or go out of business altogether.

This churning fits the picture of the struggling small business owner. Most face an uphill battle to succeed against larger and more established firms. Most small business owners have limited access to capital, little prior business experience, and few reserves to cushion against bad business decisions or a period of economic weakness. This is why most newly formed businesses do not survive for more than a few years.

The uphill struggle facing small business owners does not make life easy for their workers. Jobs at small businesses are far less secure than jobs at large

---

$1,050,000 should have little difficulty either paying the tax directly or borrowing against the value of the estate to cover the expense. Of course, the situation would be different if the entire estate were subject to the tax if it happened to cross the $1 million threshold.

[3] See "Talk of Lost Farms Reflects Muddle of Estate Tax Debate," *New York Times*, April 8, 2001.

[4] This discussion draws on data from Davis et al. (1996) and Belman et al. (1998).

employers. The average worker in a business employing fewer than 25 workers held his job for just 4.4 years, compared to 8.5 years in large firms. Workers at firms employing more than 1000 people earned an average of 17 percent more than workers at firms employing fewer than 25 people. While more than two-thirds of workers at large firms had pension coverage, only 13 percent of workers at small firms had pensions. More than 75 percent of workers at large firms had health insurance coverage, compared to less than one-third of the workers at small businesses.

The reality is that most small businesses are marginally profitable and very unstable. This makes life difficult for the employees of small businesses who are in many cases themselves trying to support families. While it is great that people have the opportunity to pursue their dreams and start a business, it is not obvious that the government should be taxing the rest of us to provide subsidies of various types to these businesses. The dreams of small business owners should not be nightmares for taxpayers and their employees.

Nanny State Subsidies for Small Businesses

There are three basic ways in which the government provides subsidies to small businesses: favorable tax treatment, below market rate loans, and exemptions from labor and safety standards that apply to other businesses. In addition, various levels of government often apply affirmative action standards for small businesses, setting aside a certain portion of their contracts for businesses that are below a specific size.[5]

The government provides tax benefits to small businesses through two mechanisms, one of them legal, and the other not quite legal. The first mechanism is a large set of tax breaks that are explicitly designed to help small businesses. Effectively, the government applies a different set of tax rules based on the size of the business. Small business owners are allowed to take many deductions, such as accelerated depreciation on capital equipment, that are not generally available to larger businesses. If a small business is incorporated – most small businesses are not incorporated so that their profits are simply taxed as the income of business owner(s) – they generally pay tax at a lower rate than larger businesses. While the tax code has become more generous to large businesses in recent years, it is even more generous to small businesses.

The other way in which the government provides tax benefits to small businesses, or, more correctly to small business owners, is by allowing them to take tax deductions for what are effectively personal consumption expenditures. While this is technically not legal, as a practical matter, millions of small business owners do not strictly separate personal expenses from business expenses. This allows them to take tax deductions for many everyday consumption expenditures.

---

5 For example, the federal government set aside $3.6 billion in contracts for the reconstruction after Hurricane Katrina for small businesses, see "FEMA Shifts Some Gulf Coast Housing Contracts From Big Businesses to Small Ones, *New York Times*, April 8, 2006.

The most obvious example of this sort of bogus deduction is a business owner who writes off a car as a business expense, even though it might have been bought primarily for personal use. This subsidy can be quite substantial. If a small business owner buys a $36,000 SUV, and is in the 33 percent tax bracket, he gets $12,000 off of his taxes under the investment tax credit for small businesses. This is more than twice as large as what a typical family would receive under TANF, the government's core welfare program.

Small business tax scams don't end with cars. Many small business owners find ways to write off vacations, computers and other home electronics, and even substantial chunks of their mortgages, all for consumer spending that the rest of us have to pay for without help from the government. Taking these sorts of tax deductions is illegal, but the conservative nanny state doesn't treat the money that it gives small business owners in undeserved tax subsidies in the same way that it treats TANF payments to poor families. While families receiving TANF payments are rigidly monitored in order to keep improper payments to a minimum, the IRS is lax in its enforcement of the rules on tax deductions for business expenses, even though the latter involve a much larger drain on the Treasury.

In addition to providing special shelter from taxes for small businesses (thereby increasing the tax burden on the rest of the working population), the government also acts as a discount banker for small businesses. The federal government, as well as state and local governments, has a vast array of loan-subsidy programs that allow small business owners to borrow money at below-market rates of interest.

The nanny state conservatives don't like to frame it this way, but a loan at below-market interest rates is just as much a subsidy as handing someone a check. From the standpoint of the government, it is losing as much money when it subsidizes a loan by charging less than the market rate of interest, as when it makes a cash payment to a family for TANF of the same amount. Both below market loans and transfer payments to low income families increase the budget deficit, the main difference being that subsidies on loans for small businesses tend to be much larger, and encounter less political resistance.

For example, as part of the recovery program from Hurricane Katrina, the Small Business Administration instituted a loan program that provided loans of as much as $1.5 million, for periods as long as 30 years, at an interest rate of less than 4 percent.[6] A loan of this size implies a subsidy of $60,000 a year. (This calculation assumes, conservatively, that the market rate of interest for these businesses would be 8 percent. Given the financial condition of the businesses likely to be receiving these loans, banks might actually demand a much higher interest rate.) This subsidy is more than 10 times as large as the cash grant that a typical family receives from TANF.

It is natural that the public would have sympathy for the business owners, many of whom faced enormous losses due to the hurricane and would not

---

[6] The terms of these "Economic Injury Disaster Loans" are described on the Small Business Administration's website [http://www.sba.gov/disaster_recov/loaninfo/ecoinjury.html].

survive without help from the government. But it was possible for these businesses to buy insurance that would have covered them against hurricane damage. They opted not to spend this money and are now asking the government to bail them out. Real believers in a free market would tell these business owners that they should have prepared and bought insurance, but nanny state conservatives support using the government to bail out small businesses following a natural disaster.

The Laws That Don't Apply

As every good conservative knows, federal, state, and local governments apply a vast array of labor, health and safety, and environmental regulations to business. What they mention less frequently is that many of these rules do not apply to small businesses. There are a wide range of exemptions or special clauses that allow favored treatment for small businesses in many statutes.

For example, the federal minimum wage does not apply to many small businesses, if they are not considered to be engaged in interstate commerce. Most states have their own minimum wage laws, but even these often have special lower rates for small businesses. For example, in Ohio, the state minimum wage for firms with over $500,000 a year in sales is $5.15 an hour, the same as the federal minimum wage. For firms with annual sales between $150,000 and $500,000 the minimum wage is just $3.35 an hour, and for firms with sales of less than $150,000 the minimum wage is just $2.80 an hour.[7] This means that a small Ohio firm that hires three full-time workers at the applicable minimum wage gets a break of more than $14,000 a year compared to what larger firms are required to pay. Most other states also have lower minimum wages for small businesses.

Special rules don't end with lower minimum wages. Most other rules regulating labor markets have provisions that ease the burden for small businesses. For example, the Family and Medical Leave Act, which requires businesses to give workers leave of up to six months to care for family members, does not apply to firms that employ fewer than 50 workers. The Consolidated Omnibus Budget Reconciliation Act (COBRA), which requires employers to allow former workers to continue to remain on a company health plan, does not apply to businesses that employ fewer than 20 people.

Small businesses even get special breaks in the enforcement of health and safety and environmental regulations. For example, the Environmental Protection Agency has special rules that allow small businesses to voluntarily report their violations of pollution regulations, and thereby escape the fines that would apply to larger businesses that committed the same offenses.[8] Other

---

[7] Information on the minimum wage rules for Ohio can be found on the CCH Business Owner's Toolkit at [http://www.toolkit.cch.com/pops/P98_05_4046_OH.asp].

[8] See the Environmental Protection Agency's "Q&A's on EPA's Small Business Compliance Policy," (revised 5/19/04) [http://www.epa.gov/Compliance/resources/policies/incentives/smallbusiness/smbfactsht.pdf].

agencies offer a similar kid glove approach towards law enforcement when it comes to violations by small business owners.

The special treatment for small businesses even extends to mine safety, a fact that came to light in Congressional hearings following a series of fatal mining accidents early in 2006. Apparently, the Mine Safety and Health Administration has a regulation that allows fines to be reduced for small or financially troubled mines.[9]

Do Small Businesses Need the Nanny State?

There is little doubt that small businesses face a difficult course in the modern economy. Larger, well-established businesses have an enormous advantage over upstarts. It is probably desirable for the government to provide assistance to small businesses to give them more of a chance. The economy and society benefit from having a dynamic business sector, where upstarts can hope to gain a toehold and introduce new ideas and products. For this reason, a good case can be made that many of the tax breaks and subsidies for small businesses are justified.

At the same time, we should not view small businesses as the embodiment of virtue. When a small business owner lies about business expenses to avoid paying the taxes that he owes, this is every bit as much a drain on taxpayers as when families file false claims for welfare benefits. It is also important to remember that many small business owners have no idea what they are doing. They may be ambitious and hard-working, but these attributes are not a substitute for common sense. It does no one a service if the government finances small business owners on ventures that are sure to fail. The employees of a doomed business will soon find themselves out of work looking for new jobs, as is likely to be the case for the business owner as well.

It is reasonable to carefully consider the ways in which small businesses are being granted special treatment. Some tax breaks and loans might be desirable, but it is difficult to see the social benefit of sending miners into an unsafe mine, simply because the mine is a small business.

But more important than the specific policies designed for small businesses is the recognition that the free market is not generally friendly to small businesses – the vast majority of small business owners are heavily dependent on the special treatment they get from the nanny state. Most small businesses are constantly struggling and usually only survive a short time. But without special treatment on taxes, loans, and regulations, even fewer would survive. While small business owners across the country like to envision themselves as tough individualists, the reality is that they are actually among the prime beneficiaries of the conservative nanny state.

---

[9] "U.S. Easing Fines for Mine Owners on Safety Flaws," *New York Times*, March 2, 2006.

CHAPTER EIGHT

Taxes

It's Not Your Money

Many nanny state conservatives seem to view taxes as voluntary contributions to the government, similar to contributions to an art museum, rather than a fee that people are required to pay in exchange for the benefits of government services. As a result, they feel the need to coddle tax evaders, giving them the opportunity to pay only as much tax as is convenient.

There is a long list of items that have come up in this vein. For example, not long after the Republicans took control of Congress, they staged hearings in which a long list of witnesses, some wearing masks to conceal their identities, recounted horror stories of abuse by the IRS. Whether or not the specific tales were true, the proposed remedies seemed intended largely to facilitate tax evasion. This effort hit its apex when the IRS came up with a plan to audit tax auditors. Under this plan, they would randomly select auditors for review to ensure that they were treating the taxpayers whose accounts they were inspecting with the proper courtesy.

Auditing the auditors would go a long way towards making tax payments voluntary. If the career civil servants in the IRS know that they risk their job by pushing suspected tax evaders too hard, the predictable outcome would be that auditors would take their responsibilities less seriously, and allow hundreds of thousands of cases of tax evasion to slip by without complaint.

This particular policy was stopped largely as a result of a little sunshine: a front-page article in the *New York Times* by reporter David Cay Johnston produced enough outrage to get the policy reversed before it went into effect.[1] Unfortunately, the reasoning behind the "audit the auditors" policy continues to permeate much thinking about tax policy. There continue to be ample opportunities to evade taxes, which many politicians seem anxious to expand. More importantly, failure to pay taxes is treated as being fundamentally different than taking money from the government in other contexts. For some reason we are supposed to be more concerned about a $5,000 check to a mother receiving TANF from the government than a clever entrepreneur who evades $500,000 in tax liability.

---

[1] "IRS Workers Face More Investigations by Treasury Agents," *New York Times*, November 18, 1999. The article on reversing the policy appeared two days later, "Official Curbs Plan to Investigate Many in IRS," *New York Times*, November 20, 1999.

Getting the Tax Accounts Straight

The attitude of the nanny state conservatives toward tax evasion can be difficult to follow for those who both pay their taxes and know arithmetic. Taxation is how the government pays for the services it provides. Taxes are not voluntary – everyone disagrees with some uses of government money – but that doesn't give people the option not to pay their taxes. Similarly, there is no perfect system of taxation and no matter how well the tax code is designed, there will inevitably be inequities. But this also does not give people the right to ignore their taxes. Furthermore, given a specific level of spending, when people avoid taxes, the burden shifts to everyone else.

Taxes can be thought of as similar to condominium fees or assessments for sewage and sanitation by a community association. Once the fee structure has been set, paying the fee is a condition of staying in a condominium or owning a house in a community. It is not optional. The money that an owner of a condominium or a house pays is not "their money," it is money owed to the larger group. It is the responsibility of the owner of the condominium or house to figure out how to pay the money. There should not be a little game whereby the condominium or community association has to entice the fees, or some fraction thereof, away from the individual owners.

In fact, from the standpoint of the owners who do pay their required fees, the fees that go unpaid are the same as money spent by the association. Both unpaid fees and additional spending force the homeowners who follow the rules to pay higher assessments. Those interested in protecting the interest of the law abiding homeowner/taxpayer should show every bit as much concern about those who evade their taxes as they do about wasteful spending.

This is not how the nanny state conservatives would have us see the world. They would have us believe that the taxes that go unpaid (disproportionately by the wealthy) are a private matter between those taxpayers and the government. In their view, the effort to collect the tax money owed to the government is an abuse of government power and a threat to individual freedom. This conservative nanny state attitude appears in both policy debates on enforcement and also in efforts to equalize tax burdens across categories of goods and services.

Enforcing Tax Laws: Why the Rest of Us Should Care

According to the IRS, in 2001 (the most recent year examined) the government lost more than $340 billion in uncollected taxes.[2] This is money that is actually owed to the federal government – not money that taxpayers have been able to legally avoid paying through creative accounting or the clever use of loopholes. This is a substantial sum. It is approximately 20 times what the federal government spends on Temporary Assistance to Needy Families (TANF) each year, the main welfare program for poor families. It is 55 times

---

[2] See "Tax Cheating Has Gone Up, Two Federal Studies Find," *New York Times*, February 15, 2006.

what the federal government spends on Head Start and almost 100 times annual foreign aid spending for Sub-Saharan Africa. Alternatively, the taxes that go unpaid each year are 30 percent of what the federal government actually collects in income taxes (personal and corporate). This means that if the federal government could find a way to get tax evaders to pay their bills, then tax rates could be reduced for everyone by 25 percent, and the federal government would have the same amount of money.

The amount of money lost through outright tax evasion would seem to be a good argument for stricter law enforcement to ensure greater tax compliance. However, many of the obvious steps that could increase compliance have been nixed by the nanny state conservatives. For example, it would be a very simple matter to have taxes deducted from interest income on bank accounts or from dividend checks just as taxes are routinely deducted from paychecks. This would ensure that the government had at least a partial payment of the tax owed on this income, and that the IRS had a reliable record of the money that taxpayers received from these sources. If the tax deducted from this income proved to be too much or too little, taxpayers would collect the difference or make up the gap when they filed their annual returns. In fact, in the eighties the Reagan administration actually put in place rules requiring that taxes be deducted from most interest bearing accounts, but more extreme nanny state conservatives in Congress got these rules reversed.

The nanny state conservatives are anxious to thwart measures that make it more difficult for wealthy people to evade taxes. In the late nineties there was an effort by the wealthy countries to crack down on money laundering, largely as a way to combat crimes such as drug running or illegal gambling. Shortly after President Bush took office, Treasury Secretary John O'Neil indicated that the Bush administration was not interested in this sort of law enforcement.[3]

In addition to outright evasion, the nanny state conservatives believe that the nanny state should give special treatment to wealthy people for a wide variety of activities. David Cay Johnston documented many practices through which the wealthy can legally avoid paying taxes in his book *Perfectly Legal*, and there is no reason to go through this list here.[4] The wide range of legal methods available for tax avoidance may not have made the income tax an entirely voluntary payment for the wealthy, but, at the least, these tax breaks offer them a substantial discount off the taxes implied by the standard tax rates.

Indulgence of tax evasion/avoidance does not extend to everyone. In recent years the IRS has been especially vigilant in policing the returns of people claiming the earned income tax credit (EITC). The EITC is a tax credit for low-income wage-earners that dates back to the Nixon administration. It was

---

[3] During the Clinton administration, the United States worked with other wealthy countries to develop a treaty to crack down on international tax havens. The Bush administration backed away from this international effort in its first six months in office. "A Retreat on Tax Havens," *New York Times*, May 26, 2001.

[4] See also the discussion of tax loopholes and mechanisms for improving enforcement in Sawicky (2006).

intended to offset the payroll tax that these workers pay for Social Security and Medicare. The maximum amount that a family could receive from the EITC in 2005 was slightly over $4,000, with most families receiving substantially less.

In 2003, approximately 19 million taxpayers filed to receive the EITC. The IRS chose to ask for detailed documentation from 4 million of these filers, more than 20 percent.[5] This level of vigilance in preventing false filings on the EITC is impressive since the most money that the IRS can retrieve, even when uncovering a totally false (as opposed to exaggerated) claim to the EITC, is just over $4,000. By contrast, just 5 percent of taxpayers reporting income of more than $1 million had their tax returns audited by the IRS.[6] If the main priority of the IRS is maximizing compliance with the tax code, its resources might be better spent tracking down some of the wealthy people responsible for the $340 billion in taxes that go uncollected each year than low-income workers who may have claimed a few hundred dollars too much on the EITC.

Will the Nanny State Allow a Level Playing Field?

The federal tax code includes thousands of quirks that allow special tax breaks that serve no obvious public purpose.[7] This section deals with two gaps in taxation that receive less attention than they deserve: allowing Internet sales to escape state and local sales tax, and taxes on financial transactions comparable to those in place in Britain and other countries. Both taxes raise issues of equity – there is no reason someone should be able to escape paying sales tax because they buy a stereo online instead of buying it at Wal-Mart. Similarly, there is no obvious reason that people who bet at casinos or on state lotteries should pay taxes on their gambling, but people who place their bets in the stock market should be exempt from taxation.

It is difficult to find any logic in allowing Internet sales to go untaxed. People who buy goods over the Internet tend to be wealthier, on average, than the population as a whole. Higher-income people are more educated and more likely to have Internet access and therefore are more comfortable surfing the web. Allowing Internet sales to go untaxed, while sales at traditional retailers are subject to state sales taxes, effectively means having low and moderate income people subsidize the purchases of the wealthier segments of the population.

The effect of this system at the level of the retailer is also perverse. Some Internet retailers, for example, Amazon.com, are multi-billion dollar operations. People who buy goods from Amazon.com don't have to pay sales tax, but if the same person goes to a neighborhood store, she would have to pay state sales tax. In effect, the system subsidies Internet retailers, regardless of how large they are, at the expense of traditional retailers, many of which are small family run businesses. There are instances in which government policy goes overboard to help small businesses, but it certainly is reasonable to suggest that small

---

[5] "IRS Tightening Rules for Low-Income Tax Credit," *New York Times*, April 23, 2003.

[6] "IRS Quickly Answers Study on Audits of Rich Americans," *New York Times*, March 29, 2006.

[7] Some examples of tax breaks that promote environmentally harmful behavior can be found on the Green Scissors Campaign website [http://www.greenscissors.org].

businesses should not have to pay taxes that their much larger competitors can avoid.

The history of efforts to extend state sales tax collection to Internet retailers provides an interesting example of how nanny state conservatives have been effective in framing issues. Internet retailing grew from nothing to a major industry in the late nineties tech bubble. At the time, there was no provision for taxing sales of firms that did business across state lines like Internet retailers. (The main precedent was retailers who did business through mail order catalogues.) In principle, the sales of these businesses are subject to the sales tax in the state where the customer lives, however, the retailer is not responsible for collecting the tax. The customer is supposed to pay the sales tax themselves on items purchased from an out-of-state retailer. Tax collections through this route are virtually zero.

If states are to collect sales tax from Internet sales, they will have to force retailers to collect taxes directly on purchases. Since states lack jurisdiction over retailers in other states, it will be necessary for federal legislation to require Internet retailers to collect state and local sales tax. When this issue first came to take on importance with the growth of Internet retailers in the late 1990s, the industry pushed the argument that Internet retailing was an infant industry that needed a period to grow, and that it should not be strangled with taxes. It wasn't clear why Internet companies needed or should be entitled to a temporary tax holiday, while any normal store would be subject to state and local sales taxes from the day they opened.

In recent years, as Internet retailing has become a staple of the economy, the argument about protecting an infant industry has largely disappeared. Instead, the Internet retailers have argued that requiring them to collect sales taxes on the wide array of goods they sell, given the huge number of taxing jurisdictions, would be almost impossible. They pointed out that different jurisdictions don't only have different tax rates, but in many cases they define items differently. For example, in some states or counties, a scarf might be a clothing item and therefore exempt from taxation, whereas other states or counties would categorize a scarf as a personal accessory (like sunglasses), and therefore subject to taxation. Internet retailers have argued that such distinctions make collecting sales taxes impossibly complex, and therefore they should not be required to do so.

The argument that adjusting tax rates for a large, but certainly very limited, number of taxing authorities is an impossible task for a cutting edge Internet retailer is quite striking.[8] In fact, coding items by zip code (which the retailers have presumably mastered), would largely be sufficient for the accurate collection of state and local sales taxes. The fact that a small fraction of the items shipped might be assigned the wrong tax rate is largely irrelevant. Some fraction of the items sold in traditional retailers also gets taxed at the wrong rate. That is not a reason for eliminating the sales tax.

---

[8] Maybe the legislation requiring Internet retailers to collect taxes can include funding for college students in computer science programs to help the retailers as part of a work-study program.

Thus far, Internet retailers have succeeded in avoiding responsibility for collecting state sales taxes. Part of their success is attributable to the fact that applying sales tax to the Internet purchases is seen as a new tax, rather than applying an existing tax to businesses that have been evading it. As long as Internet retailers succeed in avoiding state sales taxes, they will be accomplishing the important social goals of subsidizing the consumption of relatively affluent families and also making shareholders in Internet retailers wealthy. In effect, most of the profits of an Internet retailer like Amazon.com can be seen as cashing in on their special tax status. If Amazon.com were suddenly forced to pay the same sales tax as the traditional stores with whom they compete, it would have to largely absorb this tax in the form of lower profits.[9] Jeff Bezos, the billionaire CEO of Amazon.com, is yet another success story of the conservative nanny state. If Amazon.com were subject to the same tax rules as a corner grocery store, Mr. Bezos might be just another failed small business entrepreneur.

What's Wrong With Taxing Wall Street Wagers?

If a bus driver in New Jersey spends a weekend gambling at Atlantic City, she will pay a tax of 7 percent on her gambling. If she buys $100 worth of lottery tickets, then she will pay an effective tax of almost 30 percent on the gamble.[10] By contrast, if a corporate lawyer spends an afternoon buying and selling hundreds of thousands of dollars worth of the same stock in the hope of catching an upswing or downswing, she will pay almost no tax on her gamble.[11]

In the United States, most forms of gambling are subject to heavy taxation. However, if you opt to do your gambling in financial markets, the conservative nanny state allows you to largely avoid taxes, which substantially improves the likelihood of coming out ahead.

There is a long history of applying taxes to financial transactions in the United States and around the world. Every major financial market has imposed substantial taxes on transactions, and many still do. For example, the London stock exchange still imposes a tax of 0.5 percent on the sale of a share of stock. Japan had a set of relatively high transactions taxes in place until the collapse of its stock bubble. At the peak of Japan's stock bubble in the late eighties, the

---

[9] If Amazon.com could more profitably charge higher prices for its products, it would already be doing so. This means that if customers have to add sales tax to every purchase, this tax will primarily come out of profits because consumers will not be willing to pay the price of the product plus the tax.

[10] Information on New Jersey's casino tax can be found in the New Jersey Casino Control Act, Article 11, Fees and Taxes, available at the State of New Jersey Casino Control Commission's website [http://www.state.nj.us/casinos/actreg/act/article11.html]. In 2004, state governments netted a total of $15.1 billion on $47.7 billion in revenue from their lotteries (U.S. Census Bureau. 2006. *Statistical Abstract of the United States*, Washington, DC: Table 446). These tax rates are the tax rate on the amount of money that is gambled, they are not taxes on winnings. Any winnings would be subject to the income tax in addition to the tax assessed on the gambling.

[11] In fact, there is a very modest tax of 0.003 percent on stock trades. This tax raises approximately $900 million annually, which is used to finance the operations of the Securities and Exchange Commission.

government collected 4 percent of its revenue through a financial transactions tax, the equivalent of $160 billion in the United States in 2006. Even the United States used to have a substantial financial transactions tax. Trades of shares on the New York Stock Exchange were subject to a federal tax of 0.04 percent until 1964, and a state tax of 0.19 percent until the late 1970s.[12]

Given the long history of financial transactions taxes in the United States and elsewhere, the concept should not be foreign to public policy debates. Financial transactions taxes have also enjoyed the support of many of the country and the world's most prominent economists, including John Maynard Keynes, Nobel Laureates James Tobin and Joe Stiglitz, and former Clinton Treasury Secretary and Harvard University President Lawrence Summers.[13] While these economists have put forward many reasons as to why such a tax might be desirable, the basic argument is simple. People who want to buy shares of stock or other financial assets for purposes of long-term investment are not going to be much affected by a tax of less than 0.25 percent. A tax of this magnitude may discourage some short-term traders, but this could be a good thing, since short-term speculation can sometimes destabilize a market.

A modest financial transactions tax can also raise a great deal of money. A set of modest transactions taxes on sales of stocks, bonds, options, futures, and other financial instruments could raise $70 billion a year.[14] Most of this money would be raised from short-term traders. (This calculation assumes a sharp fall-off in short-term trading in response to the tax; if the volume of trading was not affected by the tax, the revenue would be even larger.) This revenue could be used to fund new public services, reduce the size of the deficit, or could even be used to reduce other taxes, if we were concerned about the government becoming too large. For example, it might be possible to reduce the 10 percent bracket in the income tax code to 5 percent, if the government raised $70 billion a year by taxing stock trades and other financial transactions.

Nanny state conservatives invariably become outraged when proposals to tax financial transactions get raised in public policy debates. It is one thing to tax the gambling that working people do at casinos or state lotteries. It is quite another to tax their gambling on Wall Street. Furthermore, many of the country's richest people get their income from operating hedge funds that rely on being able to quickly buy and sell billions of dollars of financial assets with small transactions fees. In effect, these hedge fund operators are in the same position that the Atlantic City casino owners would be in if they didn't have to pay gambling taxes to the government; pocketing the government's share of the revenue is a huge boost to profits. This also explains the intense opposition to a tax on financial transactions. For these people, applying the same sort of taxes to Wall Street gambling as the rest of the country pays on its gambling could mean an end to their very way of life.

---

[12] The history of financial transactions, taxes is discussed in Pollin et al. (2003).
[13] See Summers and Summers (1989) and Stiglitz (1989).
[14] See Pollin et al. (Table 7).

Realistically, the fears the nanny state conservatives raise over modest financial transactions taxes don't pass the laugh test. There has been a sharp fall in the fees and commissions on stock trades over the last quarter century due to improvements in technology and increased competition in the brokerage industry. A tax of 0.25 percent on stock trades probably wouldn't even raise the total cost of an average stock trade as high as its 1990 level. The United States had a robust stock market in 1990, so there seems little basis for concern that a modest financial transaction tax will somehow shut down financial markets.

No one will ever be happy about paying more money in taxes, but for the typical middle class stock investor, this tax would be a trivial burden. A person who buys $10,000 worth of stock in 2006 and sells the shares in 2016 at $20,000 would pay a total tax of $75 at the 0.25 percent rate. She would pay $25 when she buys the stock, and another $50 when she sells the stock. For the typical middle class investor, this sort of transactions tax would not be a major issue. And, if the tax on financial transactions were offset with tax reductions in other areas, most middle class investors would likely come out ahead.

In principle, the government has no reason to prefer one form of gambling to another. Wealthy people use the financial markets as the forum for their gambling in the same way that working class and middle class people use casinos and state lotteries. There is no reason to heavily tax gambling in casinos and state lotteries and allow gambling in financial markets to escape taxation altogether.

Beyond the Conservative Nanny State Tax Philosophy

The hotel heiress and convicted tax evader Leona Helmsley reportedly said that "taxes are for the little people." This could be the official motto of the conservative nanny state. While the biggest injustices of the conservative nanny state stem from the way in which it stacks the deck in favor of the wealthy in the distribution of pre-tax income, it also provides ample opportunities for the wealthy to gain further advantage when it comes to paying their tax bills. This is apparent both in the structure of the tax code and also in the resources devoted to its enforcement. Until tax evasion is treated as a serious crime in which evaders do serious jail time, it is a safe bet that many wealthy people will take advantage of opportunities to pay little or no tax.

The *New York Times* recently highlighted one such opportunity when it reported complaints from the Virgin Islands over the enforcement of a provision in the tax code. Apparently, there is a clause in the tax code that allows U.S. citizens who own a home in the Virgin Islands to pay a tax rate of just 3.5 percent on their income.[15] The island government and several wealthy beneficiaries of this tax break were unhappy over a provision that required they spend an average of 183 days a year in the Virgin Islands to benefit from this tax break. They argued that 122 days a year in the Virgin islands should be sufficient time to get the benefit of the 3.5 percent tax rate.

---

[15] "Virgin Islands Are at Center of Dispute on Tax Break," *New York Times*, March 5, 2006.

CHAPTER NINE

Don't Make Big Business Compete Against Government Bureaucrats

In the conservative nanny state mythology, the government is run by hopelessly inept bureaucrats who bury everything they touch with red tape. As a result, almost by definition the government is wasteful and inefficient. The term "government boondoggle" is redundant. By contrast, the private sector is full of hardworking, energetic, innovative people. It's the land of sink or swim; those who don't have what it takes get pushed by the wayside. The forces of competition assure us that the private sector will quickly innovate to improve quality and lower cost.

Given the nanny state mythology about the inherent superiority of the private sector to the public sector, it is remarkable how concerned the nanny state conservatives often get over the prospect of forcing the private sector to compete with the government. If they really believed what they say, the prospect of competing against the government would be a joke to American business – sort of like a middle-aged couch potato training to do battle against the young Mohammed Ali. But in this story, Mohammed Ali is scared to climb into the ring.

The Efficiency of Social Security: Simple and Old-Fashioned, Like the Wheel

In the recent debate over privatizing Social Security, proponents of privatization would often ridicule the existing Social Security system as being an old-fashioned one-size-fits-all program. They were largely right in their description, but they were wrong about its implications. The Social Security system might be 70-years-old and simple in design, but it is also cheap to operate. The administrative costs of the Social Security system are less than 0.5 percent of the tax revenue that it takes in each year.[1] By comparison, the administrative costs of the privatized Social Security systems that were held up as models for the United States, like the ones in Chile and Britain, are between 15 - 20 percent of annual payments into the system.[2]

In fact, the difference in costs is even greater when the cost of issuing annuities – turning the money accumulated in private accounts into a monthly

---

[1] Data on the administrative expenses of Social Security can be found in the 2005 Social Security Trustees Report, Table III.A6, available at
[http://www.ssa.gov/OACT/TR/TR05/III_cyoper.html#wp83991].

[2] For the information on the administrative costs of the privatized Social Security system in the United Kingdom, see Murthi, J., P. Orszag, and M. Orszag. 1999. "The Charge Ratio on Individual Accounts: Lessons from the U.K. Experience." Birbeck College Working Paper 99-2, University of London. For a discussion of the administrative costs in the privatized systems in Latin America, see Gill et al. (2005).

flow of income in retirement – is factored into the equation. Private insurers charge fees that range between 10-20 percent of the accumulated funds for issuing annuities.[3] This means that the share of workers' payments into private accounts that get eaten up by fees from the financial industry can run as high as 30-40 percent. Fees of this size will substantially reduce the amount of money that workers have left for retirement. By comparison, the administrative costs of Social Security, at less than 0.5 percent, is a bargain.

There is no mystery as to why Social Security is so much cheaper to administer than private sector funds. First, it doesn't have to market itself. One advantage of a single centralized system is that everyone is in the system, it is not necessary to chase after customers to bring them into the system. In countries with privatized systems, huge numbers of sales people are employed to market the system to potential customers. A second reason is that there are no high-paid executives in the Social Security system. The system is run by civil servants. The people at the top end earn decent salaries, but no one is getting paid hundreds of thousands of dollars that high-level executives earn in the private sector, and certainly not the multi-million dollar salaries that are now standard for CEOs in the financial sector. Social Security also doesn't have to pay dividends to shareholders out of fees charged to workers.

Finally, the simplicity of Social Security itself saves on administrative costs. While private funds allow, and even encourage, people to shift their money back and forth between different funds, there are no individual investment funds to maintain at Social Security. In private funds, workers can spend long periods of time on the phone tying up themselves and employees switching money back and forth between investment options. In the case of Social Security, most workers have little contact with the agency between the day they get their Social Security card and the day that they start collecting benefits.

The fact that there is little choice involved with Social Security is actually a virtue. Social Security is not like a car, a house, or clothes where people want to be able to decide for themselves what they will buy. The program is designed to provide workers a guaranteed core retirement income. The simplest way in which this core income can be provided is the best way. By this standard, the privatized systems can't come close to matching the efficiency of Social Security.

Of course, workers want the opportunity to have additional income in retirement beyond Social Security. Historically, employer-based pensions were the primary mechanism through which workers supplemented their Social Security income. However, traditional employer-provided, defined-benefit pension plans, which guarantee workers a monthly benefit based on their wage income, are rapidly disappearing. In 2005, just 21 percent of workers in the private sector had a traditional defined benefit plan, down from almost 40

---

[3] On the cost of issuing annuities see Poterba and Warshawsky (1999).

percent in 1980[4]. This number is certain to shrink further in the near future as employment dwindles in sectors of the economy that still have defined benefit plans and as companies that did offer defined benefit plans, convert to defined contribution systems.

This is where the efforts of the Social Security privatizers can be instructive. President Bush's 2001 Social Security commission examined the possibility of establishing a nationwide system of individual accounts as a partial replacement for the guaranteed benefit provided by Social Security. They recognized the high administrative costs associated with the existing system of defined contribution pensions in the United States, as well as the costs of privatized Social Security systems in other countries. In order to reduce the costs of a privatized system, they proposed having a single centralized system which would pool workers' savings from all over the country. Their proposal called for having a limited number of investments options (e.g. a stock index fund, a bond index fund, a money market fund, and possibly one or two other options) and limited opportunities to switch between funds.

According to the Bush commission's estimates, the administrative costs of this bare-bones system would be approximately 5 percent of the money paid into the system. While this is still very expensive compared to the 0.5 percent in administrative fees charged by Social Security, it is far less than the 15-20 percent in fees charged by financial firms for operating private sector defined contribution pensions in the United States, or that financial firms charge to operate privatized Social Security accounts in other countries. The Bush commission also assumed that the centrally managed system they proposed would be able to convert the money accumulated in these accounts into annuities at no cost. This would save workers fees of 10-20 percent, compared to a situation in which they had to buy annuities from insurance companies.

While the Bush commission may have been overly optimistic in its assumptions about the cost of operating a centrally managed system of individual accounts (especially the part about no cost for converting accounts into annuities), it was certainly correct that a publicly run, centrally managed system can administer accounts for a much lower cost than private financial firms charge. Given the potential for savings on administrative fees, it would seem an obvious gain in efficiency to create a system of low-cost centrally managed individual accounts, just like those proposed by the Bush commission, but have them be a voluntary supplement to Social Security, rather than a replacement for Social Security.

If such a system were established, workers could have considerably higher retirement incomes, at no cost to the taxpayer. The gains would come entirely from the savings on the administrative fees charged by the financial industry. For example, if a worker saved $2,000 a year for 30 years, and kept the money in a typical 401(k) type account, he would have approximately $95,000

---

[4] Data for 2005 can be found on the "Get Detailed Statistics" section of Bureau of Labor Statistics website [http://www.bls.gov] (Employee Benefits Survey). Historical data can be found in Mishel et al. (2005, Figure 2G).

accumulated at the point when he retires (adjusting for inflation).[5] By contrast, if a public system can be run at the cost assumed by President Bush's Social Security commission, then this worker would have accumulated $107,000 under the centralized public system.

Gains from a government-run system would be increased still further if the account is annuitized, turning their accumulations into a lifelong flow of income. If financial firms charged an annuitization fee of 15 percent, then the accumulation in the 401(k) would translate into a monthly payment of approximately $370. By contrast, if the government-managed system could actually convert accounts into annuities at no cost, as claimed by the Bush commission, then the same worker would get a retirement income of $490 a month with the same contribution under a government run system. The combined savings on annual fees and annuities would raise workers' retirement income by more than 30 percent.

In fact, a government-run system of accounts could even go one step further. In defined pension systems the worker incurs market risk. The worker has both the risk that she will make the wrong investment decisions and also that the stock market will slump just at the point where she is prepared to retire or prepared to withdraw her money from the stock market. Bad luck or bad judgment can leave workers with a considerably worse standard of living in retirement. While firms have been unwilling to accept this market risk themselves (which is one reason that they have been quick to turn defined benefit plans into defined contributions plan), there is no reason that the government cannot assume this risk.

The government is well positioned to average returns over good and bad years, offering workers benefit payments higher than market returns allow in periods when the market is in a slump, while providing a return lower than the market rate during a period in which the stock market is unusually strong. In effect, the government could offer workers a voluntary defined benefit pension by accepting the market risk that private sector firms are either unwilling or unable to accept.

The basic formula is very simple. The government could project an average rate of return on the basket of assets its fund will hold. For example, assuming a mix of 60 percent stocks and 40 percent bonds, it could assume that the fund's before-expense return will average 4 percent.[6] The government can then effectively guarantee this rate of return and promise a pension that is

---

[5] This calculation assumes an average real return of 4.0 percent, before deducting fees. It assumes that the fees on a standard account average 1.0 percent of the amount on deposit. This assumption about administrative costs may be somewhat low. A slightly dated study from the Department of Labor estimated that the administrative costs of 401(k) plans average 1.4 percent of the money on deposit. See U.S. Department of Labor, 1998, "Study of 401(k) Fees and Expenses," Pension and Welfare Benefits Administration, Table IV-6.

[6] This assumes that stocks will provide an average real return of 4.8 percent a year and that bonds will provide an average real return of 3.0 percent. These figures are consistent with the bond return assumptions in the Social Security trustees report and the stock returns that would be consistent with the trustees projected rate of profit growth (see Baker et al. 2005).

directly related to the worker's contribution over her lifetime. In this sort of defined benefit system, the worker who contributes $2,000 a year to her pension for 30 years, as discussed earlier, would be *guaranteed* a retirement income of $490 a month at age 65. This guarantee would be independent of how the market actually performs during this 30-year period. The government would be assuming the risk, rather than the worker.

This sort of voluntary defined benefit system would set a schedule whereby every worker would be able to guarantee herself a specific, inflation-adjusted annuity at retirement, based on the contributions made at various ages. Money deposited at older ages would provide less income in retirement since the deposit would have compounded less interest, while money deposited earlier in life would guarantee a higher monthly payment since it would have compounded more interest.

The system could also allow workers to start drawing their pension before age 65 in exchange for a reduced monthly benefit (adjusted for both the longer number of years over which the benefit would be collected, and the shorter period of time that the money would have earned interest) or after age 65 in exchange for an increased monthly benefit. There would be other complicating factors as well. For example, there should be provisions for dual-life annuities for couples, and possibly payments to survivors for workers who die before reaching retirement age.

It is not important to lay out specific details of a voluntary national defined benefit system at the moment. The key point is that it is possible to design such a system, and that it would likely offer many advantages over the retirement accounts currently available through the private financial system. In fact, there is no reason that the government could not offer both a system of defined benefit and defined contribution pensions side-by-side, with individuals deciding for themselves how much money, if any, they want to contribute to each.

This could be done on an entirely voluntary basis. The only requirement that would be necessary from the government is that employers allow workers to make deductions from their paychecks into the public pension system, as is now done with 401(k) type accounts. Employers could have the option of making contributions on workers' behalf, or setting up various matching arrangements, as many do now with defined contribution pensions.[7]

A national system like this would mean that every worker in the country at least would have the option of contributing to a pension (both defined contribution and defined benefit) at his or her workplace. At present, just over half the workforce has access to a pension at the workplace, and the vast

---

[7] It might also be desirable to have some default contribution (e.g. 3.0 percent of wages) to the retirement system that would be deducted from workers' paychecks unless they explicitly requested that it not be deducted. Recent research indicates that workers are more likely to contribute to a pension plan if contributing is the default option than if not contributing is the default option (see Gale et al. 2006). Even if the default is that workers contribute, the plan would still be entirely optional, since workers could request that their money be paid out in full in wages.

majority of these pensions are defined contribution pensions. In addition, the pension would be fully portable, so workers could stay in the same pension throughout their working lives regardless of how many times they changed jobs or where in the country that they happened to move.

The proponents of individual accounts, who were singing the virtues of savings and the "ownership society" during the debate over the privatization of Social Security, should jump at this opportunity to facilitate individual savings and allow workers additional choice in where they can invest their savings. The real problem with the country's retirement system is not Social Security. It is the private pension system and the lack of individual savings. This system of universal voluntary accounts would go far toward addressing this problem.

Can a Little Government Competition Fix the Health Care System?

The United States health care system is seriously broken and getting worse by the day. Much attention has been given to the fact that 43 million people are not covered by health insurance. The United States is the only developed country that doesn't guarantee health care insurance for its citizens. But this is the less serious part of the problem. The United States spends more than twice as much per person as the average for other wealthy countries, yet our health outcomes (measured by life expectancy or infant mortality rates) put the United States near the bottom of the list among wealthy countries. (The fact that so many people in the United States believe that it has the best health care system in the world, in spite of the overwhelming evidence to the contrary, is a testament to the power of the industry lobby and to the poor job the media has done of informing the public about the health care system.) People in the United States are projected to live on average 2.3 fewer years than people in Canada and 3.9 fewer years than people in Japan. Table 9.1 shows the OECD's estimates of per-person health care costs and life expectancy for the wealthy countries.

As bad as the picture in Table 9.1 appears, the real problem is that the situation in the United States is getting worse. Health care costs are rising more rapidly than the overall rate of inflation. Health care costs consume approximately 16.2 percent of GDP, or just over 16 cents for every dollar of output. In 10 years, the share of the economy devoted to health care is projected to rise to 20.0 percent of GDP.[8] Health care spending is projected to continue to rise more rapidly than GDP long into the future. The projections for disastrous budget scenarios 20 or 30 years into the future, that are widely cited by fiscal conservatives, are driven primarily by the assumption that health care costs are not contained.[9]

---

[8] These projections are taken from the Center for Medicare and Medicaid Services (2006, Table 1).

[9] See for example Peterson (2004 and 1999). See also, Baker, D. 2004. "Medicare Choice Plus: The Answer to the Long-Term Deficit Problem," Washington, DC: Center for Economic and Policy Research [http://www.cepr.net/publications/medicare_2004_03.htm]. This paper describes a plan that would substantially reduce the burden from Medicare costs by giving

Table 9.1

International Comparisons:
Life Expectancy and Health Care Costs

	Life Expectancy at Birth (1999)	Per Capita Cost PPP (2001)
Australia	79.0	$2,513
Austria	78.1	$2,191
Belgium	77.6	$2,490
Canada	79.0	$2,792
Denmark	76.6	$2,503
Finland	77.4	$1,841
France	78.8	$2,561
Germany	77.7	$2,808
Greece	78.1	$1,511
Iceland	79.6	$2,643
Italy	79.0	$2,212
Japan	80.6	$2,131
Netherlands	77.9	$2,626
New Zealand	78.3	$1,710
Norway	78.4	$2,920
Spain	78.6	$1,600
Sweden	79.5	$2,270
United Kingdom	77.4	$1,992
Non-U.S. Average	**78.4**	**$2,295**
United States	**76.7**	**$4,887**

Source: OECD Health Care Statistics, 2004.

beneficiaries a voucher that allows them to buy into the health care system of any country with a longer life expectancy than the United States. The savings, which would eventually run to more than $45,000 a year per beneficiary, would be divided between Medicare, the beneficiary, and the foreign government selected by the beneficiary.

Since the government pays for approximately half of the country's health care costs through Medicare, Medicaid, and insurance plans for current and retired government employees, if health care costs follow the projected trend path, then they will have a devastating impact on federal and state budgets.[10] However, if health care costs follow this projected trend, they will also have a devastating impact on the private sector. Companies that continue to cover most of their workers' health care costs will be at a serious competitive disadvantage with firms in other countries that incur only a fraction of the expense to cover workers' health care costs. Many businesses will opt to stop insuring their workers, or will only pay a portion of their workers' insurance, forcing them to pay the rest out of their paychecks. In this context, the percentage of the population that is uninsured is virtually certain to grow substantially.

In order to prevent a dysfunctional health care system from devastating the economy and leaving an ever larger segment of the population uninsured, it is essential that the health care system be reformed in a way that contains costs – a feat that every other wealthy country in the world has managed to accomplish. Some of the problems driving health care costs can be addressed by policies discussed in prior chapters. For example, the United States pays it doctors on average more than twice as much as doctors receive in other wealthy countries. If the United States allowed free trade in physicians' services, opening the door to qualified doctors from around the world, salaries in the United States would adjust to world levels, saving close to $100 billion a year in health care costs.

The fastest growing portion of health care costs is spending on prescription drugs. This is attributable to the fact that the United States (alone among developed countries) awards pharmaceutical manufacturers unrestricted patent monopolies. If the research costs for drugs, and also medical instruments such as MRI scanners, were paid up front through public funds, and all innovations were then placed in the public domain, drugs and medical equipment and supplies could be sold in a competitive market. This would lead to savings of close to $200 billion annually compared to the current patent monopoly situation.

However, even with these changes, the United States would still stand apart from the rest of the world due to the huge amount of money that we spend on administering the health care system. The system of competing private insurers adds enormously to the cost of the health care system. The direct cost of administering the insurance industry is equal to approximately 12 percent of the country's health care bill.[11]

---

[10] The extent to which these projections are driven by the assumption of exploding health care costs is shown in Baker, D. and D. Rosnick, 2003. "The Forty-Four Trillion Deficit Scare." Washington, DC: Center for Economic and Policy Research [http://www.cepr.net/publications/deficit_scare.htm].

[11] See Woolhandler and Himmelstein (2002).

By comparison the cost of administering Medicare is less than 3 percent of the cost of the services it provides. For many of the same reasons that Social Security is an efficient provider of retirement income for the country's workers, Medicare is an efficient provider of health care to the country's senior citizens. Operating as a single centralized system, Medicare doesn't have to incur the same sort of marketing expenses as private insurers to get and keep customers. It also doesn't pay the seven and eight figure salaries that top executives receive in HMO's and other private sector health care providers. In addition, it doesn't have to pay out profits to shareholders.

Other countries have administrative costs for their health care system that are comparable to those of the Medicare system. In addition to the costs of operating the insurance industry, the U.S. system also imposes costs on health care providers. Since each insurer will have its own set of forms and reimbursement schedules, hospitals, nursing homes, doctors' offices, and other health care providers must employ staff who can deal with all the various forms with which they are presented. This additional administrative expense is equal to approximately 19 percent of national health care spending, making total administrative expenses in the United States approximately 31 percent of health care spending.

The amount of waste implied by this number is partially concealed by the size of the denominator. Per person health care expenditures in the United States are more than twice as high as the average for developed countries. There is no reason that administrative costs should necessarily rise in proportion to health care costs. On a straight per person basis, the United States spends approximately 80 percent as much for administering its health care system as Britain spends running its health care system. Per person administrative costs in the United States are equal to 60 of per person health care expenditures in Canada. This is serious waste.

The Route to Containing Administrative Costs

The obvious way to get the administrative costs of the U.S. health care system in line with other developed countries is to adopt the sort of universal system – effectively a universal Medicare system – that low administrative cost countries like Canada have in place. The proposal to overhaul the current system of private insurers and replace it with a government run system will naturally send the nanny state conservatives into near hysteria with cries of "socialized medicine."

There is a simpler route. The government could simply open the Medicare system on a voluntary basis to any employer or individual who wanted to sign up.[12] The Medicare program could charge standard insurance rates based on age, and compete with existing private sector plans.[13]

---

[12] Hacker (2002) has a version of this proposal.

[13] It would be necessary to include provisions to prevent gaming of the system. For example, to prevent people from signing up for a low cost plan if they are healthy, and then switching to

It is likely that the vast majority of employers and individuals not insured through an employer would quickly sign up with a Medicare-run plan.[14] The savings in administrative costs would allow Medicare to provide better service to patients at a lower price. In addition, its already enormous size gives Medicare the bargaining power to push down the price it pays to health care providers for medical services. This gives Medicare a further advantage compared with private sector insurers.

In addition, employers would have a degree of certainty with Medicare that they do not have with private sector plans. Private sector plans often impose large year-to-year price increases either because of rising costs generally (or reduced competition) or in an effort to recoup costs from a business where one or more employee has a serious illness. While businesses can shop among insurers to find a lower rate, it is a time-consuming process, especially for small businesses with limited managerial capacity. If a business had the opportunity to sign up with Medicare, it would have the security that its premiums would never take a large jump. Premiums for any specific business would follow the national path in health care costs.

The opportunity to save money immediately and to ensure that costs will not rise unpredictably in the future is likely to be welcome to most businesses and individuals. For this reason, if the option to join Medicare was extended to the country as a whole, it is likely that most businesses and individuals would quickly sign up. This may not immediately bring the country to universal coverage, but it would substantially reduce the number of uninsured and create a mechanism for bringing health care costs under control.

What's Wrong With Giving People a Choice?

There are very good reasons to believe that a national centralized system can provide pension and health insurance coverage more effectively and at lower cost than existing private financial firms or health insurance providers. But it is not necessary to speculate as to which system will provide better service. If the public sector option is made available, the decision can be left to the market. Businesses and individuals would be free to choose the system that they felt best met their needs, at the lowest cost.

If the nanny state conservatives believe what they say, they should not be concerned about the risk that public sector pension and health insurance systems will pose to private plans. In fact, the prospect of competing against the government arouses great fear among nanny state conservatives. This was one reason the Republican Congress explicitly prohibited the Medicare system from offering its own prescription drug benefit in the 2003 law establishing a Medicare drug benefit.

Medicare once they become sick, there can be a provision that charges substantially higher fees to firms or individuals who sign up after an initial period of open enrollment.

[14] It would be necessary to include a system of subsidies to low income families, with the government paying most, or all, of the premium, in order to achieve universal coverage.

The same logic has led providers of wireless Internet service to run to state legislatures across the country to pass laws prohibiting cities from offering their own wireless Internet service, as is being done in San Francisco, Philadelphia, and other major cities. There are good reasons to believe that wireless Internet service can be most efficiently provided through the public sector – or at least through a single provider acting under contract with the government. The logic is straightforward. Once a network is established, it can be readily expanded to accommodate almost any number of people. It is likely to be cheaper to have a single wireless network that carries all the traffic in the area than to have many networks that duplicate service, each carrying a small amount of Internet traffic.

In the case of wireless Internet service, as with a voluntary national pension system and an open enrollment Medicare system, the issue is simply one of choice. No one is suggesting a prohibition on private Internet providers, private savings accounts, or private health insurance plans. The question is whether to provide a government run option in competition with the private sector. In this situation, the nanny state conservatives are strongly opposed to giving people a choice. They want the nanny state to ensure hefty profits for the financial industry, the health insurance industry, and Internet service providers even if means higher prices, poorer service, and a less efficient economy.

Beyond the Conservative Nanny State

Political possibilities look very different if we move beyond the nanny state conservatives' framing of the world. They do not want us to even discuss the really important factors that determine who gets rich and who ends up poor: Federal Reserve Board policy, free trade for doctors and lawyers, copyrights and patents. Once we insist that everything must be placed on the table, it is easy to design policies that offer substantial rewards in terms of higher growth and will also lead to a more equal distribution of income.

Freeing trade in professional services should be an easy one. The economic gains from having free access to doctors and other professionals from India, China, and other developing countries vastly exceed the potential gains from trade deals like NAFTA and CAFTA that make the "free traders" so excited. The savings on these services will make health care much more affordable and make other prices lower, effectively raising the real wages of the workers who are already facing competition from workers in developing countries.

One key economic fact that the nanny state conservatives understand very well, and that confuses many progressives, is that one person's income is a cost to another person. Nanny state conservatives clearly recognize that when they make the wages of autoworkers and nannies lower, they make themselves richer, because the goods and services produced by autoworkers and nannies will cost less. The exact same logic applies to the wages of professionals. When their wages fall, the goods and services they produce will cost less to everyone else. Lowering the wages of doctors, lawyers, economists, and journalists is not just beating up on relatively well-paid workers, it is also increasing the real wages of dishwashers, autoworkers, and nannies. Progressives must recognize this simple fact of economics and arithmetic if they want to understand public policy.

As noted in Chapter 1, allowing free trade in professional services can also be a boon to developing countries. It is simple to design a mechanism for taxing the earnings of foreign professionals in the United States, which would allow the country of origin to educate two or three professionals for every one that works in the United States. This sort of tax is also essential to ensuring a healthy flow of professionals from the developing world, because in the absence of compensation, developing country governments will not use public resources to train their students to work as professionals in the U.S. market. This flow of tax revenue would be in addition to the remittances that many foreign-born professionals would voluntarily send to friends and family members in their home countries.

In short, free trade in professional services is a great win-win-win proposition. It enhances economic growth in the United States while redistributing income downward, it enhances economic growth in developing countries, and it provides a great opportunity for advancement to the foreign-

103

born professionals themselves. The nanny state conservatives have already made the arguments for free trade. All we have to do is substitute "doctors" and "lawyers" for "cars" and "clothes" and add a couple of zeros to the projections of economic gains.

Of course, many people may not want to subject some or all of our highly paid professionals to global competition. Perhaps they think it is important that doctors earn more money in a month than restaurant workers earn in a year. Preserving the protection that allows such inflated salaries is a political decision that the public will have to make. But it is important that the public be well-informed in deciding the matter. The difference between the average doctor's salary in the United States and the average in Europe is approximately equal to annual TANF grant of 20 welfare recipients.[1] This is money in the form of tax dollars (through public sector health care programs like Medicare) and higher health care premiums that is being pulled out of workers pockets and given to doctors. If the public determines that higher income for doctors is a good use of their money, then they are of course free to support the government protections that ensure these high incomes.

It is also important to cleanse the public debate of nonsense rhetoric concerning protectionism. The United States has a large body of laws and regulations that protect important segments of the workforce, raising prices for the services from these sectors by hundreds of billions of dollars annually. There is no economic theory whatsoever that says that protection for cars and clothes is harmful to the economy, while protection for doctors and lawyers is harmless. The economic damage caused by protectionist measures depends primarily on how much they raise prices. The measures that sustain high wages for doctors, lawyers, and accountants have far more economic impact and do far more harm to the economy than most of the protectionist measures that have been proposed for textiles, steel, or other manufactured goods.

Full-employment monetary policy from the Fed should also be front and center on our policy agenda. It is not acceptable to tell millions of people that they must go jobless just because some inflation fighting Fed chair wants to stage a pre-emptive strike against potential inflation. Inflation can pose a problem, but unemployment definitely does pose a problem, especially when the burden of higher unemployment is disproportionately borne by those at the bottom of the social-economic ladder. It is reasonable to argue that any balancing of the costs and benefits should lean more heavily towards risking higher inflation.

It is also important to remember that costs are not incurred only by those who are unemployed. The way in which unemployment counteracts inflation is by putting downward pressure on the wages of the segment of the workforce most vulnerable to unemployment: less educated workers, and racial and ethnic minorities. When it raises interest rates to combat inflation, the Federal Reserve

---

[1] The gap in pay between an average doctor in the United States and a doctor in Europe is approximately $100,000 a year. This is 20 times the average cash TANF grant, which is approximately $5,000 a year.

Board (an agency of the government) is trying to reduce the bargaining power of these workers, forcing them to accept lower pay and benefits than they could command in an economy with higher levels of employment. While higher unemployment may be helpful in containing inflation, we should remember that it is also a redistributive policy, taking from those at the bottom and middle of the income distribution and giving to those at the top.

Given the enormous costs of higher unemployment, it is reasonable to look for alternative mechanisms to contain inflation. Other countries have had success with centralized bargaining processes as a way of keeping wage growth from pushing a wage-price spiral. There is no easy way to transport this system to a country like the United States, with low unionization rates and no real history of centralized bargaining. But since the losses from the excess unemployment used to contain inflation run into the hundreds of billions a year, it is worth some effort exploring possible alternative mechanisms that could accomplish the same end. In the quarter century following World War II most economists thought that some type of wage-price guidelines/controls could be effective in containing inflation. In spite of the current conventional wisdom within the economic profession, it is possible that the earlier generation of economists was not completely wrong.

If it turns out that our economists are not smart enough to think of a less expensive way to contain inflation that produces less human suffering, we should at least be aware of the sacrifices that the unemployed are making on our behalf. It is their suffering that is restraining wage growth for tens of millions of other workers, thereby allowing the economy to continue to grow without excessive inflation. At the very least, the unemployed deserve some recognition for the sacrifice they endure so that the rest of us can enjoy economic prosperity.

This brings up a third issue that should be central on any progressive agenda: national health care insurance. There is overwhelming public support for some type of national health care insurance, since few people believe that the uninsured should just be left to die when they get a serious illness. The argument for national health care insurance becomes even stronger when we consider that as a matter of government policy, millions of people might be forced out of work. Since most health insurance is provided through employers, and most of the unemployed lack the resources to pay for insurance themselves for any substantial period of time, it seems the least that we could do for them – in exchange for their efforts to keep inflation under control – is to provide them and their family with health care insurance.

Even if there is general support for the idea of national health care insurance, transitioning from the current system to a system of universal health care insurance is not an easy task. Health care costs have been out-of-control for decades, and efforts to extend public sector coverage are soon overwhelmed by the decline in private sector coverage due to ever-rising costs. Unless the system is transformed and costs are contained, there is no way to provide universal coverage.

As discussed in Chapter 9, the market may well provide an answer to this problem. If we allowed every employer and individual in the country to voluntarily buy into the Medicare program, we would be building on the most efficient component of the nation's health care system. An expanded Medicare program would allow employers to buy into a plan that offers lower costs than most private insurers, due to both its low administrative expenses and also its ability to negotiate price reductions with health care providers. Employers could also be assured that Medicare would not send their rates soaring if an employee developed a serious illness. While buying into Medicare would be voluntary, if the system is properly structured it is likely that most employers would quickly go this route to insure their workers. Individuals would have the same option to buy into Medicare.[2]

By itself, this would not be sufficient to achieve universal coverage. It would be necessary to have some additional subsidies in place that would pay for much or all of the insurance costs for low- and moderate-income families. But this is very much a doable task once the basic structure is in place. If the country has a health care system in which costs are contained, the public sector can provide the funds needed to insure those who cannot afford to pay for their own insurance. On the other hand, if costs continue to grow along the path currently projected, it is inevitable that the number of uninsured will rise through time, even if there is an expansion of public sector health care programs.

There is one other point about the importance of reversing conservative nanny state policies that redistribute income upward. In a period of stagnant or declining real wages, the public will be very resistant to efforts to raise taxes to support more public services of any type. On the other hand, in a climate of rising wages and general prosperity, there is less objection to diverting a portion of this prosperity towards meeting public needs. This means that if the economy is producing real gains for the bulk of the population, it will be much easier to obtain the revenue needed to address deep-seated social problems.

Moving Beyond the Conservative Nanny State Framing

The three policies described above – a trade policy focused on opening trade in high-end professional services, a full employment monetary policy, and national health care insurance – would go far towards reversing the growth in inequality in the United States over the last quarter century and insuring a decent standard of living for the entire population. Many of the other policies discussed in prior chapters could also go far toward both increasing economic growth and reducing inequality. However, the specific policies put forward in this book are less important than the framework for understanding policy.

The nanny state conservatives have been incredibly successful in structuring the political debate over the last quarter century. They have laid out

---

[2] As discussed in Chapter 9, there would have to be rules in place that would prevent the gaming of the system, for example, by not paying for insurance while healthy, and then signing up after developing a serious health condition.

a framework in which they are perceived as wanting the market to control major areas of the economy and society, while their liberal and progressive opponents want the government to take control. The nanny state conservatives have succeeded in having the key forms of government intervention that shape the market pulled off the table, so that they are never discussed. The liberal/progressive opposition is then left to cry for the helping hand of government to reverse market outcomes, rather than trying to reconfigure the rules to produce a different set of outcomes. Many progressives even use the phrase "market fundamentalist" as a term of derision directed against conservatives. Such attacks must delight the intellectual defenders of the conservative nanny state, since nothing suits them better than having discussion of the rules that redistribute income upward taken off the table.

As this book has argued, it is ridiculous for progressives to embrace a position that puts the government acting in the public interest in opposition to the market. The market is an incredibly powerful force. Good policy seeks to harness it in ways that produce desirable social outcomes. It is much easier to have the river flow in the right direction, than to try to block its path and have it flow backwards. The nanny state conservatives have spent the last quarter century putting in place a set of policies and rules that ensure that the river flows in a way that sends income upwards. If these rules are not challenged, then it will be impossible to design policies that ensure that the bulk of the population enjoys a decent standard of living.

It is also ridiculous to claim that conservatives don't like government or that they don't run it well. It is true that conservatives don't like big government social programs, but that is because they want to redistribute income upward and big government social programs are designed to provide security for the entire population. But conservatives are enthusiastic supporters of the big government policies that send income flowing upward, and they are quite effective in running the sectors of government that bring about this end.

In the Reagan and Bush administrations (as was also the case in the Clinton administration) there were no serious problems with foreign doctors or other highly paid professionals practicing in the United States and competing down the wages of U.S. professionals, as the government quite effectively limited such competition. The Fed has been quite successful on several occasions in raising interest rates and keeping millions of people from holding jobs. Pfizer, Microsoft, and Time-Warner have been able to have their patents and copyrights successfully enforced not only in the United States, but increasingly across the globe, as U.S. trade negotiators have forced other countries to provide stronger patent and copyright protection in recent trade agreements. The nanny state conservatives even gave the government an enhanced role as a bill collector in the bankruptcy law that Congress passed in 2005.

The reality is that the nanny state conservatives want a big role for the government in the economy and they are very effective in managing the government when it comes to having it do the things that they care about. They might not do a good job in saving the people of New Orleans from a hurricane, but saving poor people is not the agenda of the nanny state conservatives. Their agenda is making sure that no one mass produces copies of Windows without Microsoft's permission. Enforcing this type of monopoly, and other interventions that distribute income upward, is the role for government preferred by the nanny state conservatives, and the government performs these functions very well under their watch.

In addition to being essential for the effective design of government policy, reframing the debate is also crucial for the prospects for political success. The basic point is very simple: if progressives argue their positions using a script written by conservatives, then we lose. If we argue about "free trade" agreements, which have as one of their primary purposes increasing patent and copyright protection, then we start with a huge disadvantage. Even worse, progressives will sometimes talk about restricting drug patents (as in requiring compulsory licensing for essential medicines) as a form of interference with the free market. The hearts of the nanny state conservatives must be filled with joy when they hear their own rhetoric spouted passionately from the mouths of their political opponents.

The nanny state conservatives have largely been running the political show in the United States over the last quarter century. This is due in part to the fact that the liberal/progressive opposition has been so incredibly confused in trying to lay out an alternative framework. At the moment, there is nothing on the table that passes the laugh test in either its policy coherence or political appeal.

In order to have any hope at succeeding, we will have to move beyond the political framing of the nanny state conservatives. Many people have become comfortable with the framing "we like the government, they like the market," but it is both wrong and politically ineffective. If liberals/progressives insist on adhering to this framework, then they guarantee themselves continuing failure in the national political debate. This framing would be fine if the point is to simply show up and be the perennial losers of national politics, but if the point is to actually change the world in a way that makes it better for the bulk of the population, then we must be prepared to move beyond the ideology of the conservative nanny state.

REFERENCES

Anderson, G., P. Hussey, B. Frogner, and H. Waters. 2005. "Health Spending in the United States and the Rest of the Industrialized World," *Health Affairs*, 24, no. 4: 903-914.

Baker, D. 2005a. "Opening Doors and Smashing Windows: Alternative Measures for Funding Software Development," Washington, DC: Center for Economic and Policy Research. [http://www.cepr.net/publications/windows_2005_10.pdf]

Baker, D. 2005b. "Are Copyrights a Textbook Scam? Alternatives to Financing Textbook Production in the 21st Century," Washington, DC: Center for Economic and Policy Research. [http://www.cepr.net/publications/textbook_2005_09.pdf]

Baker, D. 2004. "Financing Drug Research: What Are the Issues?" Washington, DC: Center for Economic and Policy Research. [http://www.cepr.net/publications/intellectual_property_2004_09.htm]

Baker, D. 2003. "The Artistic Freedom Voucher: An Internet Age Alternative to Copyrights," Washington, DC: Center for Economic and Policy Research. [http://www.cepr.net/publications/ip_2003_11.pdf]

Baker, D., B. DeLong, and P. Krugman. 2005. "Asset Returns and Economic Growth," *Brookings Papers on Economic Activity*: 289-315.

Baker, D., A. Glyn, D. Howell, and J. Schmitt. 2004. "Unemployment and Labor Market Institutions: The Failure of the Empirical Case for Deregulation," New York: Center for Economic Policy Analysis. [http://www.newschool.edu/cepa/publications/workingpapers/archive/cepa200404.pdf]

Bebchuk, L. and Y. Grinstein. 2005. "The Growth of Executive Pay," *Oxford Economic Papers*, 21, no. 2: 283-303.

Belman, D., E. Groshen, J. Lane, and D. Stevens. 1998. *Small Consolation: The Dubious Benefit of Small Business for Job Growth and Wages*, Washington, DC: Economic Policy Institute.

Bernstein, J. and D. Baker. 2004. *The Benefits of Full Employment*, Washington, DC: The Economic Policy Institute.

Blackford, M. 1998. *The Rise of Modern Business in Great Britain, the United States, and Japan*, Chapel Hill, NC: University of North Carolina Press:. 38-40.

Burke, T. 2002. *Lawyers, Lawsuits, and Legal Rights: The Battle Over Litigation in American Society*, Berkeley, CA: University of California Press.

Calem, P. and L. Mester. 1995. "Consumer Behavior and the Stickiness of Credit-Card Interest Rates," *American Economic Review*, 85, no. 5: 1327-1336.

Center for Medicare and Medicaid Services. 2006. *National Health Care Expenditure Projections: 2005-2015*, Washington, DC: Center for Medicare and Medicaid Services. [http://www.cms.hhs.gov/NationalHealthExpendData/downloads/proj2005.pdf]

Congressional Budget Office. 2006. *The Budget and Economic Outlook, 2007-2016*. Washington, DC: Congressional Budget Office. [http://www.cbo.gov/ftpdocs/70xx/doc7027/01-26-BudgetOutlook.pdf]

Congressional Budget Office. 2003. *The Economics of Tort Liability: A Primer*. Washington, DC: Congressional Budget Office. [http://www.cbo.gov/showdoc.cfm?index=4641&sequence=0&from=0]

Davis, S., J. Haltiwanger, and S. Schuh. 1996. "Small Business and Job Creation: Dissecting the Myth and Reassessing the Facts," *Small Business Economics*: 297-315.

Dew-Becker, I. and R. Gordon. 2005. "Where Did the Productivity Growth Go? Inflation Dynamics and the Distribution of Income." *Brookings Papers on Economic Activity* 2005: 2.

DiMasi, J., R. Hansen, and H. Grabowski. 2003. "The Price of Innovation: New Estimates of Drug Development Costs." *Journal of Health Economics*, 22: 151-185.

Ernst & Young LLP. 2001. "Pharmaceutical Industry R&D Costs: Key Findings about the Public Citizen Report." Pharmaceutical Research and Manufacturers of America. [http://www.cptech.org/ip/health/econ/phrmaresponse.pdf]

Freeman, E. 2003. "Barriers to Foreign Professionals Working in the United States," Washington, DC: Center for Economic and Policy Research. [http://www.cepr.net/publications/professional_supplement.htm]

Friedman, J. 2004. "Administration Tax-Cut Rhetoric and Small Business," Washington, DC: Center on Budget and Policy Priorities. [http://www.cbpp.org/9-28-04tax.pdf]

Galbraith, J. 1998. *Created Unequal: The Crisis in American Pay*, New York: The Century Foundation.

Gale, W., J. Gruber, and P. Orszag. 2006. "Improving Opportunities and Incentives for Saving by Middle- and Low-Income Households," Washington, DC: Brookings Institution. [http://www.brookings.edu/views/papers/200604hamilton_2.htm]

Gill, I, T. Packard, and J. Yermo. 2005. *Keeping the Promise of Social Security in Latin America*, Stanford, CA: Stanford University Press.

Goldstein, M. 1998. *The Asian Financial Crisis: Causes, Cures, and Systematic Implications*. Washington, DC: Institute for International Economics: 26-44.

Hacker, J. 2002. *The Divided Welfare State: The Battle Over Public and Private Social Benefits in the United States*. New York: Cambridge University Press.

Himmelstein, D., E. Warren, D. Thorne, and S. Woolhandler. 2005. "Illness and Injury as Contributors to Bankruptcy," *Health Affairs*.
[http://content.healthaffairs.org/cgi/content/abstract/hlthaff.w5.63v1]

Horwitz, M. 1997. *The Transformation of American Law, 1780-1860*. Cambridge, MA: Harvard University Press.

Johnston, D. 2003. *Perfectly Legal*, New York: Portfolio Publishers.

Krugman, P. 1995. "Voodoo Revisited." *The International Economy*, November-December.

Lowes, T. 2005. "Exclusive Survey: The Earnings Freeze, Now It's Everybody's Problem" *Medical Economics*, September 16.
[http://www.mcmag.com/memag/article/articleDetail.jsp?id=179086&].

Mishel, L., J. Bernstein, and S. Allegretto. 2005. *The State of Working America, 2004-05*. Ithaca, NY: Cornell University Press.

Murthi, J., P. Orszag, and M. Orszag. 1999. "The Charge Ratio on Individual Accounts: Lessons from the U.K. Experience." Birbeck College Working Paper 99-2 (University of London).

Peterson, P. 2004. *Running on Empty: How the Democratic and Republican Parties Are Bankrupting Our Future and What Americans Can Do About It*, New York: Picador.

Peterson, P. 1999. *Gray Dawn: How the Coming Age Wave Will Transform America and the World*, New York: Crown.

Pharmaceutical Research and Manufacturers of America. 2005. *Pharmaceutical Industry Profile 2005*, Washington, DC: PhRMA.

Pollin, R., D. Baker, and M. Schaburg. 2003. "Security Transaction Taxes for U.S. Financial Markets," *Eastern Economic Journal*, 29, no. 4: 527-558.

Posner, R. 1986. *The Economic Analysis of the Law*, New York: Aspen Publishers.

Poterba, J., and M. Warshawsky. 1999. "The Costs of Annuitizing Retirement Payouts From Individual Accounts." Cambridge, MA: National Bureau of Economic Research Working Paper 6918.

Sawicky, M. 2006. *Bridging the Tax Gap: Addressing the Crisis in Federal Tax Administration*. Washington, DC: Economic Policy Institute.

Summers, L. and V. Summers. 1989. "When Financial Markets Work Too Well: A Cautious Case For a Securities Transactions Tax," *Journal of Financial Services Research*.

Stiglitz, J. 1989. "Using Tax Policy to Curb Speculative Short-Term Trading," *Journal of Financial Services Research*.

U.S. Food and Drug Administration. 2001. "NDAs Approved in Calendar Years 1990-2001 by Therapeutic Potentials and Chemical Types," December 31. [http://www.fda.gov/cder/rdmt/pstable.htm]

Woolhandler, S. and D. Himmelstein. 2002. "Paying for National Health Insurance—and Not Getting It," *Health Affairs*, 21, no. 4: 88-98.

ABOUT THE AUTHOR

Dean Baker is a macroeconomist and co-director of the Center for Economic and Policy Research in Washington, DC. He is co-author of *Social Security: The Phony Crisis* (with Mark Weisbrot, University of Chicago Press, 1999), co-author of *The Benefits of Full Employment* (with Jared Bernstein, Economic Policy Institute, 2004), and author of *The History of the United States Since 1980* (Cambridge University Press, forthcoming 2006). He received his Ph.D. in economics from the University of Michigan. His blog, *Beat the Press*, provides commentary on economic reporting.

938605